PENGUIN BOOKS
16 SWIPES, THE OTHER PERSPECTIVE

Mark Powell is a British-born novelist, playwright, and screenwriter who lives in Singapore. As an explosive writer and storyteller, Mark delivers brutally realistic fiction with strong characters and compelling plots. Though his preferred genre is action/thriller, he also writes non-fiction.

His best known works include the novels *Quantum Breach* (2009), *Deep Six* (2010), *The Somali Sanction* (2012), and *16 SWIPES No Breakfast* (2019). He has also written a young adult fiction called *The Adventures of Danny Dare* (2013).

His screenplay 'The Wax Men', which is an intense political thriller inspired by a true story, and set in Hong Kong, was considered for production.

This latest book, *16 SWIPES The Other Perspective*, takes a humorous look at the world of online dating through the eyes of sixteen women and demonstrates his versatility, sensitivity, and humour as a writer. Follow Mark Powell on Instagram at markpowellauthor2.

16 SWIPES
THE OTHER PERSPECTIVE

16 Women's Adventures through Tinder

Mark Powell

PENGUIN BOOKS
An imprint of Penguin Random House

PENGUIN BOOKS

USA | Canada | UK | Ireland | Australia
New Zealand | India | South Africa | China | Southeast Asia

Penguin Books is part of the Penguin Random House group of companies
whose addresses can be found at global.penguinrandomhouse.com

Published by Penguin Random House SEA Pte Ltd
9, Changi South Street 3, Level 08-01,
Singapore 486361

First published in Penguin Books by Penguin Random House SEA 2021

Copyright © Mark Powell 2021

All rights reserved

10 9 8 7 6 5 4 3 2 1

The views and opinions expressed in this book are the author's own and the
facts are as reported by him which have been verified to the extent possible,
and the publishers are not in any way liable for the same.

ISBN 9789814914208

Typeset in Adobe Garamond Pro by Manipal Technologies Limited, Manipal

This book is sold subject to the condition that it shall not, by way of trade or
otherwise, be lent, resold, hired out, or otherwise circulated without the
publisher's prior consent in any form of binding or cover other than that in
which it is published and without a similar condition including this condition
being imposed on the subsequent purchaser.

www.penguin.sg

Dedicated to the men who partake in online dating, who it seems just got it so wrong . . .

Contents

Foreword — ix
Men Are From Mars — xiii
Life — xxi

Two's a Company, Three Is Just Weird — 1
Allow Me to Pause — 8
Dick Pic Warrior — 14
Sharing Is Not Caring — 19
Being Too Nice — 24
Mr Allergy — 31
Odour Most Foul — 36
Fashion Victim — 41
The Science of Love — 47
The American Somalian — 54
The Serial Swiper — 59
Captain America — 65

Romeo	70
Catch Me if You Can	76
True Lies	80
Ironman	86
Bonus Swipe 1: Awaken the Queen	90
Bonus Swipe 2: Excuse Me	99
Bonus Swipe 3: We Are Who We Are	109
Bonus Swipe 4: Classic Love Versus Tinder	117
Bonus Swipe 5: Shock Factor	125
Bonus Swipe 6: When One Is Not Enough	132
Bonus Swipe 7: The Shameless Cougar	144
The Good Seem to Evade the Perfect	155
The World Will Become Female	162
To Sum It All Up	169
What Women Want	175
Looking Back	181
Glossary & Terminology Guide	192
16 Swipes All Pride	202
Acknowledgments	205

VIEWPOINT

Foreword

The truth is, that I would feel like I was attacking a soufflé with a pickaxe if I were to start hacking around for deep themes, dark images, and hidden implications in this book. I didn't have to do this to find insight, wisdom, useful information or humour. Powell offers the reader fantastic nuggets of knowledge, which are peppered throughout this book, in the form of chapters that not only recount the stories of the ladies he interviewed, but also gets us—the reader—thinking. He skilfully draws in themes and research from our social interaction with each other, and in between tells us the stories of the 16 women this book showcases and honours.

Maybe it's possible to make something of the hilarious moral qualities Powell ascribes to clothing. Why does he present David as 'mould-stained and wearing a deplorable old singlet'? When we first meet David, is it important that we are treated to the sight of a 'beefy, average height, somewhat arrogant man, not gleaming in a spotless shirt of irreproachable fit'?

If this were Shakespeare, I'd be looking for great significance in the similar descriptions that run throughout the book. But in

Powell, it's just his way of humorously describing the variety of men these women have met. And, he does it so spot-on! I think it's fair to assume that the only thing that really matters here is that these sartorial notes are funny and help chronicle the world these ladies found themselves in. Safe not least because burrowing any deeper would ruin the humour in this book.

I also can't resist quoting the description one of the ladies made in summing up her date with a man who had bad body odour. Powell's words made me chuckle hard. He writes, 'The odour was so foul, in fact, it would make a rotting fish smell like the sweat of an angel.'

Few writers are better at moving characters around the various scenes, even if a few better writers make them do sillier things. Their complexity is part of their charm, and it's no surprise that Powell said:

> 'It's the plots that I find hard to work out sometimes. It can take me a long time. But when I do, the ink simply flows.'

What is even more surprising is that he then added:

> 'I like to think of some scenes over a glass of whiskey—it doesn't matter how crazy—and work backwards and forwards from it until eventually it becomes quite plausible and fits neatly into the story. Maybe the whiskey helps!'

Plausible! That's almost as funny as his intentional jokes. The other delight of the scenes that Powell creates is that it is almost entirely, gloriously absurd. But still. If you want to know how to construct a story, there are definitely worse places to look than his work.

For a humorous novel to work, you've got to have a scenario. And you've got to test it so that you know where the comedy comes in, where the situations come in, know where to split it up into scenes—you can make a scene out of almost anything—and have as little stuff in between as possible. Again, it's all but impossible to find anything 'in between'. All the descriptive action takes place in clear, discrete scenes and each one leads to the other naturally and easily and with remarkable precision. It's lean. It's heading somewhere. You get drawn in fast.

How wonderful it was to be in the presence of a master writer. Such writing cannot be equalled by just anyone. I wouldn't recommend that anyone should try. I'd also attempt to conceal—but I can't—from budding authors the horrifying information that Powell wrote 20,000 words of this quality in just two days and wrapped up the entire novel in a matter of months! In fact, *16 SWIPES The Other Perspective* should be compulsory reading for creative writing classes around the world.

Though I don't want to go deep, there are still things to say. But I will leave it to Powell to take you on this journey of dates as recounted by the ladies he spoke with. This book is cloaked in gems. It is written with respect and is masterfully done. You feel like you are sitting right there with Powell talking to the sixteen ladies.

Carol Jennings
The Shameless Cougar mentioned in this book.
September 2020

INTRODUCTION

Men Are From Mars

It is said that 'men are from Mars, and women are from Venus'. Dr John Gray's beautifully written book by the same name is undoubtedly an incredible read in my opinion, which puts forth numerous strategies for reducing tension in relationships and creating more of that stuff we crave—love. It talks about how men and women are different. It then offers practical suggestions on how to reduce levels of frustration and disappointment, that if not addressed could send a relationship on a downward spiral. In short, it shows us how to create ever-increasing happiness and intimacy.

Common sense really—relationships don't have to be such toil or struggle. It's only when we don't understand one another that issues surface, and we face tension, resentment, and conflict. Having said that, before entering into a relationship, it is first necessary to *meet* the life partner! These days it is not so much left to chance, via a physical encounter. The use of online dating sites and downloadable applications, or 'apps', have made this 'meeting' process much easier. Even if you are not looking for a relationship and just want something casual instead, it is possible using these online channels. Let us use this form of encounter as the cornerstone to delve into this book.

When Tinder first launched in 2012, it was an instant success. It was an overnight sensation that made over a million matches in less than two months. From college campuses to office towers in every city, this dating app gained recognition from tech's most elite. Within six years after its launch, the company was valued at around $3 billion, and it is one of the highest-grossing apps of all time. With a pedigree that creditable, it was enough for the 16 women featured in this book to give it a shot. Love, it seemed, could now be found in an app.

It's no secret that dating apps like Tinder and others—too numerous to mention—have made meeting new people easier than ever. But with every right swipe you make comes the potential for something to go seriously right, or very wrong—particularly since it's not uncommon to hear of a match made in online heaven quickly turn into a first date from hell. Stories of successes seem to be getting more elusive. But as it is in life, there are good and bad experiences. So, for a second, let's put aside the idea that people only go on dating apps to hook up. Sure, there are people who are looking more for experiences than relationships, and everyone has their own rational preferences when it comes to dating. Some people still crave and search for that fairy-tale romantic vibe, while others would rather have somebody, they can regularly spend time with, with no strings attached.

This book is a sequel to my own documented encounters on Tinder, titled *16 SWIPES No Breakfast*. I have shared my own experiences in the hope of making people laugh, cry, and realize that if it could happen to me, it could happen to them too.

But what was my biggest takeaway? I learnt that one of the biggest differences between men and women is how they cope with stress. Yes, I know there are many differences, but this is what I want to call out. We men can often become increasingly focused and withdrawn when under stress. I would like to emphasize here that this is, of course, *not* a generalization of the entire male—or female—species, and we are not all stereotypes, but a general observable trend. Women, on the other hand, can often become increasingly overwhelmed and emotional when stressed. During these times, a man's need for feeling better are different from those of a woman. While the male feels better by solving problems, the female feels better by talking about problems. Not understanding and accepting these differences between the two sexes creates unnecessary friction in our relationships.

Let's look at an example where I will stand in for the man.

When I reach home after a long day, I want to relax and unwind by quietly reading the newspaper, hitting the gym, or maybe watch some TV and sip on a glass of wine. I'm stressed given I have some unsolved problems at work. And I find some relief in focusing on other things and forgetting my work problems. At least, until I return to work the next day.

My wife, Jane, also wants to relax and get away from her stressful day. She, however, chooses to find an outlet by talking about the problems of her day. Tension begins to build between us and gradually it gives way to resentment.

I think to myself that Jane talks too much, while Jane feels I am ignoring her. Without understanding our differences, we grow further apart.

You can probably recognize this situation because it is just one of many examples where men and women are at odds.

It is a very common problem in most relationships. So, how should one solve such a problem? I can assure you that love alone will not solve it. It very much depends on the degree of understanding of the opposite sex.

Without stereotyping and taking a view for the sake of argument, I would like to put forth that a woman may prefer to talk about her problems to feel better, while a man would simply feel that his better half talks too much and resist listening to her! To make things worse, he may be busy doing his own thing in order to feel better, and unwittingly lead the woman into feeling ignored and neglected. As such she might persist in trying to get him to talk when he didn't want to.

But all is not lost. These two differences can be resolved by first understanding in greater detail how men and women typically cope with stress. To put it in a nutshell, men retreat, while women like to talk. So, one or the other should compromise or better still, both must meet in the middle. Give the woman in your life time to talk and in return, you can hit the lazy boy for an hour or two. Simple really.

This example is important, as in all honesty I didn't really understand or appreciate this at the time I used to go on dates. I simply did not appreciate that sometimes women think differently to men and are without a doubt from Venus!

But all said and done, I'm a male, so *16 SWIPES No Breakfast* was written through the lens of a male perspective. So, to add some moral balance I wanted to write a similar book, only this time from the female perspective. With this objective in mind, I have added a few chapters on life—what women want in a true sense and a few stories focused on how to deal with the challenges life throws at us from time to time.

I started my research by reaching out to as many female friends as I could, in the hope they had Tinder stories to share. Some did, and some did not. Many, in fact, looked at me in disgust as if to say why would you think I would have such a story to share. Funny . . . as I'm sure I 'spotted' them on Tinder more than once! Anyway, the word soon got out, and before long friends of friends and friends of those friends' friends and even complete strangers began to contact me with their stories. One lady I interviewed, avowed that her best Tinder date felt like a film from the 1960s. She described it in these words: 'When a couple walks on a beach hand in hand with nothing but the sound of waves crashing on the sand. It was magical, a real Hollywood meet cute.' In case you have no idea, what this means, it is a reference to Kate Winslet who starred in a movie titled *The Holiday with Jack Black and Jude Law*. On a separate note, do watch it—you will see what I mean.

Another, said of her date, 'It was as if I was invisible to him as a human being, and I was nothing more than a piece of meat for him to toy with.'

Dianne had finished with Tinder for the night. She had swiped right on every profile that fell within her visual preferences—a total of 250! By the morning, forty-five of them had matched with her, and Dianne agreed to go on a date with one of them. Fortunately, Dianne found her date endearing, and they are now happily married. If there is a better example of fate or luck, I can't think of one right now. Tinder had worked. Dianne had clearly not wanted to leave anything to chance and had played the odds. Today, Tinder, it seems, has put in place an algorithm to penalize those who swipe right on everyone. Sadly, the odds have now reduced.

The common thread that ties together the 16 women I feature in this book—some amicably divorced, others going through savage divorce proceedings, while a few who were separated from their husbands, simply wanted some fun—many just wanted a second chance. But above all, like Dianne, they all wanted to find their Mr Right, their shining knight in armour. Failing that, just a plain old Mr Nice Guy would suffice. But could one stumble across such a man on Tinder? The population of 'nice guy' profiles has now been tainted by scammers and players.

So, with that dream in mind, this book bears testament to the adventures—or misadventures—in today's technological and online dating scene. The fact is that it is not easy to take the plunge into this whirlpool we call dating. And doing so in your forties and fifties for a woman is even harder. Some of these women had young children, so priorities often had to be balanced. Family first, dating second. But being happy, having a shoulder to cry on, someone to talk to over dinner and simply to live a happier life, was equally important to these ladies.

I thought long and hard about it if this book should be written and couldn't decide until a lady friend—over lunch one Sunday—was telling me she had read my first book, *16 SWIPES No Breakfast*. Thankfully, she loved it, related to it and wanted to tell her own story. Even better, she had a group of friends that wanted to do the same. That was the moment I felt compelled to write the other perspective, the female view, in the hope that their experiences will help motivate and inform others that they are not alone in their desire for rediscovering love and prioritizing themselves for a change. They are not the only ones tired of loneliness. Perhaps it's more about the desire for companionship. And, if nothing else, simply just to have a good laugh.

Interestingly, women seemed to enjoy my first stories more than men and looking back at these now, I have no idea how I survived the many challenging experiences. In contrast, men want to read the female point of view. Fortunately, we now have some balance. Both sides can now be told.

To set the backdrop, the names of many of the women mentioned in this book are, of course, aliases. This is in order to protect the identities of those who graciously lent their stories and have long given up on dating for one reason or another. Hanging around in bars or clubs like a pack of hyenas—aka their girlfriends—in the hope that a suitable man may just wander in is no longer a priority for them. In the rare instance, they did see a possible catch—and he smiled back—it was usually the type of man who was simply looking for one night of fun.

So, why then did they choose Tinder as their search buddy?

For exactly the same reason a billion others have tried it—it is simple, non-confrontational, and straightforward. What is not so easy, however, is finding someone genuine among the thousands of fake profiles and scammers. It requires patience, good fortune, and smartness to do so. It also requires a great deal of lady luck!

Blind dates were a no go, and paying a fortune to join some elite dating company that proclaimed success in finding you a match over lunch, coffee or bagels, and assured levels of profiling to weed out the weirdos—which, of course, they never do—was equally not for these ladies. One lady, Claire, that did brave these elite waters and who had parted with $10,000 for the privilege and a guaranteed twelve dates, or her money back, discovered to her horror that she was being used as live bait! Yes, that's right, as bait!

One of her dates confessed, after having sipped far too many cocktails, that he had been matched with a series of less than attractive and suitable women. Given this, he was about to cancel his subscription when his account manager suggested he meet with Claire. Claire was described as attractive, and he would not be disappointed. She was simply used to keep clients happy who were on the verge of cancelling their subscription. No prizes for guessing what Claire did next, other than a lawsuit against the agency, and she had her money and costs refunded in full. Not surprisingly, Tinder was definitely worth a try for these ladies. The stage for romance would be set, and they just had to sail through the sunset. Perfect, it sounded so easy.

Many experiences later—here I am sharing their stories. It's the perfect follow-up to the male view of *16 SWIPES No Breakfast*. The ladies now have their say. And, just so I am clear—these stories are meant to be entertaining, and I hope each story offers some insight into the challenges and experiences these women endured. As far as I know, all these ladies are happy today. Some have found love. Others are happier being single, living alone, and in the company of good friends.

The dictionary defines 'online dating' as:

> A way of starting a romantic relationship on the internet, by giving information about yourself or replying to someone else's information.

Ah . . . if only things were as simple as they seem.
But, then again, where would all the fun be, if it were!

REFLECT

Life

Before we dive into the stories, allow me to offer my view on life. It sets the context of how you should, perhaps, consume the narrative that follows.

Some of the most memorable lessons in life come from stories. Stories be they fiction or true are fundamental to the way we process life experiences and the feelings that surround them. Stories are a way to encapsulate life's memorable moments and enduring lessons. The human brain is programmed to perceive patterns and grasp the plot and sequences of stories to store them in long-term memory.

I strongly believe that good stories can change lives—for the better. In fact, we know this to be true. This book is full of stories that changed the lives of those telling them. Maybe not in a big way, but change happened anyway. Allow me now to share something I found to be profound. I think it will help you understand some of the ladies who recount their dating experiences in this book. So, read on, and I hope you appreciate my point.

A gentleman was walking through an elephant camp in Thailand, and he noticed that the elephants weren't kept in cages or chained. All that was keeping them from escaping the camp was a small piece of rope tied to one of their legs. As the man looked at the elephants, he was flabbergasted as to why they didn't just use their strength to break the rope and escape the camp. They could easily have done so, but instead, they remained where they were. Curious and wanting to know why, he asked a trainer working nearby his burning question.

The trainer replied, 'When they are very young and much smaller, we use the same size rope to tie them and, at that age, it's enough to hold them. As they grow up, they are conditioned to believe they cannot break away. They believe the rope can still hold them, so they never try to break free.'

The only reason the elephants weren't breaking free and escaping from the camp was that over time they adopted the belief that it just wasn't possible.

So, what? You may ask? Consider for a moment, perhaps over a chilled glass of wine, the moral of the story. No matter how much the world tries to hold you back, always continue with the belief that what you want to achieve is possible. Believing you can become successful is the most important step to actually achieving it. With this in mind, allow me to share one more story before we continue to the swipes.

Hundreds of years ago in a small Chinese village, a small business owner owed a hefty sum of money to a loan shark. The moneylender was a very old, unattractive guy that just so happened to like and want the business owner's daughter. He decided to offer the businessman a deal that would completely wipe out the debt he owed him. However, there was a condition—in return the businessman would offer his daughter's hand in marriage. But this proposal was not met with happiness. The young girl meant everything to the businessman.

The loan shark then offered a solution. He said that he would place two pebbles into a bag, one white and one black. The daughter would then have to reach into the bag and pick one out. If it was black, the debt would be wiped out, but the loan shark would then marry the girl. If it was white, the debt would also be wiped out, but the daughter wouldn't have to marry and they could both go in peace.

Standing on the pebble-strewn path of the businessman's garden, the loan shark bent over and picked up two pebbles. As he was picking them up, the daughter noticed that he'd picked up two black pebbles and placed them both into the bag. He then asked the daughter to reach into the bag and pick one. It seemed that the daughter had three choices to choose from.

1. Refuse to pick a pebble from the bag.
2. Take both pebbles out of the bag and expose the loan shark of cheating.
3. Pick a pebble from the bag knowing it was black and sacrifice herself for her father's freedom.

The young woman drew out a pebble from the bag, and before looking at it, 'accidentally' dropped it in the midst of the other pebbles on the path. Then she said to the loan shark, 'Oh, how clumsy of me. Never mind, if you look into the bag for the one that is left, you will be able to tell which pebble I picked.'

The pebble left in the bag was obviously black, and as the loan shark didn't want to be exposed as a cheat, he had to play along as if the pebble the daughter dropped was white and clear her father's debt.

The moral of this story is that it's always possible to overcome a tough situation by thinking out of the box, and not give in to the only options you *think* you have.

So, in the world of dating and in life, in general, try to find your way out of certain situations, always believe in yourself, and think out of the box. You always have more options than you think. With that, let us begin swiping!

SWIPE 1

Two's a Company, Three Is Just Weird

So, if I asked you what an alternative lifestyle is, how would you respond? Perhaps you would suggest a certain way of eating, or how you balance your work life with your home life, or for the more adventurous, the image of something far weirder and wild, with consenting adults pretending to re-enact famous battle scenes dressed as Romans or leather-glad men or women who like to dominate their partners like a scene out of *Fifty Shades of Grey*. Regardless of your response or preference, a more generalist definition of an alternative lifestyle is a lifestyle that is considered diverse from that of a mainstream one, or generally perceived to be outside the cultural norm. So you see while it is perfectly fine to dress up as a Roman legionnaire and tramp through fields of mud at the weekend and scream 'Hail Cesar!', it is probably not the most common way of viewing this way of life.

To begin this story. There were two sets of numbers that Jane consistently cared for and watched like a hawk. And, in her mind, they were inextricably linked.

The first was her bank balance—nothing unusual in that. Her parents had taught her early in life the value of money and instilled in her the idea that freedom meant to be financially secure.

The second figure was, surprisingly, the number of Tinder matches she acquired each day. While other Tinder swipers may not see that as a barometer to keep a watch on, no one else must have obsessed about it like Jane did. Or, if they had, they probably didn't provide a running commentary to their friends in quite the same way that Jane did.

Jane wanted a man—someone to share her life with given she had been a corporate slave for far too long. It also meant a future and a future she feared spending alone. In May of 2019, one of Jane's Tinder swipes, No. 3 to be exact, matched.

It was around 5.30 p.m. on a Friday when Jane left the office and climbed into a taxi bound for home. Just as her eyes closed for a few moments of peace—after what had been a harrowing day of meetings and tolerance and smiling nicely at people who she'd have liked to vomit over—she received a *Ping* on her phone. It was a distinctive *Ping*, given it signalled that she had a match on Tinder. Jane had now become familiar with the sound, having received twenty-four of them in the past. She thought this was probably due to the fact that she had uploaded a new profile picture—one which was certainly more provocative than her previous 'yoga sweats' pose. This one cheekily presented her in a bikini, straddling a jet ski in Thailand. Normally, Jane would be greeted shortly after the *Ping* with a superficial message. 'Hello babe.' Or worse, 'Fancy sex tonight, dear?'

Jane, by way of introduction, is a forty-two-year-old English brunette who worked in PR. By any reasonable standard, she classified as being an attractive woman—given her clear complexion, green eyes, toned body, and 1.7 m height. Having worked in PR, it had made her an extrovert and each year she blew her Myers Briggs' profiling test out the water for being high on the E-scale, which meant she could hold her own at any social occasion and easily communicate verbally with anyone capable of a response. Jane literally could get Rain Man to hold a conversation. It was also Jane's fifth year spent as an expat in Singapore, having divorced her husband for cheating on her with a work associate three years ago. Finding another woman's thong tucked under the cushion of your family room couch was not something most women would tolerate. Jane had duck taped it to the fridge to let her wayward husband know she had found it. Nice touch Jane.

As such, Jane was ready to find love again, or at least some fun in the form of a nice guy to wine and dine with. Accepting offers for one-night stands for sex was not on her agenda or her bucket list. She wasn't as keen to leave her thong anywhere soon.

Jane scanned the Tinder match she had just received. Brian by way of his own profile described himself as fifty-two years old, American, physically fit, and adventurous.

His photograph suggested that perhaps he had been a little bit generous with his physical description, given it showed him gloriously posing in a pair of beach shorts—no shirt, stomach protruding, with his arm strung around another well-proportioned man in some exotic location. Jane decided to overlook his *belly of beer* on account that the photograph seemed to be at least genuine and natural. She waited no longer and sent off an introductory message. It was a discreet message in that Jane wanted to convey she had a brain and was a woman of substance and not for rent by the hour.

'Hi Brian, thanks for the match. So, if you could meet anyone in history to inspire you, who would you choose?'

Jane waited for the reply, which came some fifteen minutes later.

'Bill Gates.' Was the short and simple reply.

The banter this triggered continued for a week, with what Jane noticed as longer gaps between replies. That aside, the replies from Brian were always well-considered and written well. But undeterred by the days in between replies, Jane drew a breath and went for it. It was time to meet Brian—and his belly—face to face. She considered somewhere social, busy, and close to her own location.

After fixing up the time, date, and venue for the meeting with Brian, Jane went about her daily life that included drinks one evening with clients. The rooftop bar selected for the occasion was vibrant and relaxed. A stuffy US bank wanted some PR services set around their support of a local charity, and Jane was to lead the campaign. A very typical work event for Jane, apart from the more than friendly looks she attracted from one of the hosts of the event. John, a man in his mid-thirties, athletically built and smartly turned out in a grey suit and white shirt, was making it very clear he had a liking for her. Jane was looking equally sharp in black pants, high-heels, and a crisp white blouse. Jane cast a smile and decided to be social by making an approach. Needless to say, some banter was exchanged, and they shared numbers at the end of the evening. For professional reasons, given fraternizing with a client was a no-no in her career, it was done with discretion. John, by evidence of his business card, was a big swinging somebody with a CEO title.

A week later, Jane was on a high on the day of meeting Brian. She had closed the account with the bank seeking PR services, which may have had something to do with the fact she had, had cocktails with John a day or two after meeting him. Not that they engaged in sex. Jane made a point of telling me that it was purely professional—of course it was Jane, it mattered little to me either way!

Jane had an all-round good day and left work on time to make it home, pretty herself up, and shoot a much-needed Gin and Tonic to ease the edge of anxiety. Meeting a stranger, no matter how confident one is, is always tinged with a streak of apprehension. Even Jane's extrovert nature had at times bouts of nervousness.

Having reached and entered the bar, where she had agreed to meet Brian, a fashionable ten minutes late, Jane scanned the tables and barstools. She observed that they were populated by a dozen or so mixed and same-sex couples enjoying each other's company. Ironically, no single people were obvious. Jane looked again for Brian. Come on, we have all been in this situation. Entered a bar to meet someone for the first time and looked for that lonely soul in the corner nursing their iPhone or a drink. We standout like a leper at a health convention! Anyway, Jane had just deduced that Brian was clearly running late until a man seated off to her left stood up and waved frantically. It was Brian.

'Hi!' He boomed, and then approached like a lumbering bear.

'Hi, Brian.' Jane replied, while looking towards the table Brian had left and observing a woman, thirties, in a black dress, seated at the same table. Jane then had to ask. 'Sorry, are you busy?' She assumed the lady was a friend of Brian's or even a business meeting that had run late.

'No, not at all. Come over and I will introduce you.' Brian seemed perfectly at ease. Given that, Jane got up and moved over to their table and apprehensively took a seat and introduced herself. Meanwhile, Brian had ordered drinks.

'Hi, I'm Jane.' She extended a hand to the lady.

'Hi, I'm Joan.' Hands were shaken and drinks arrived a few moments later.

'So, Brian tells me you are in PR. What fun.'

'Yes. It can be very challenging. And you?' Jane enquired.

'Oh, I'm a domestic CEO,' Joan replied.

Jane was no fool but wanted to clarify, and in reply asked Joan if that meant a housewife. Joan laughed and confirmed yes, it did.

'So how do you two know each other?' Jane asked, having observed that Joan was making no signs of leaving the two of them alone.

The response she received in return was enough to turn Jane to pure stone.

'I'm Brian's wife.' Joan replied matter-of-factly.

Jane did a double-take, mouth turning dry.

'I'm sorry—is this a joke?' Looking at Brian and then back at Jane and then back at Brian. Brian finally spoke.

'No. My wife likes to observe me flirting with other women. We do this once a month. It's our alternative lifestyle.' Brian said, as if all were perfectly normal.

Jane took a moment.

'Strangely no . . . it is not alright.' Was all she could muster.

'Oh. Well, maybe give it a try.' Brian responded and was now seriously in danger of being slapped firmly across his smiling face.

'Did you honestly not think to mention this? I mean, what woman would be okay with this Brian?' Jane stood up.

Joan then added insult to injury. 'Oh, many are.'

Jane left with not another word spoken.

Needless to say, within minutes Brian was deleted, blocked, and forgotten for all time.

Jane has now added to her questions—should she date a man from Tinder again. 'Are you married or into three's a company. If you are, please pass me by.'

Happily though, Jane went on to find Mr Nice Guy. Yes, Mr CEO Banker man, but not before meeting a few more strange men from Tinder. But she, at least, recounts her story from a place of happiness now.

SWIPE 2

Allow Me to Pause

The No. 1 secret for achieving more success, happiness, and freedom in your life—many a keynote speaker has said—is to develop a core set of personal rules to live by, or as I prefer to call them— 'principles'.

Now this may sound counter-intuitive, but many who have adopted this belief have built seven-figure businesses in countless different industries. So it may be argued that having a set of personal principles, actually works. I certainly believe it does, and my reason is simple. Principles give you a foundation on which you can live your life to the fullest. They eradicate indecision, temptation, and distraction and, paradoxically, create more freedom for you to do the things you love. When you take the time to develop your own rules to live by, everything in life becomes easier. You no longer need to 'think' about the decisions and opportunities that come your way. Instead, you have a clear set of operating principles that you can rely on unfailingly. For example, if you don't hit the snooze button (and you truly live by that!), you never have to lie in bed and negotiate 'just five more minutes' with yourself. You wake up, turn off your alarm, and get to work. Period.

In Dani's case, she had a set of principles against which she assessed each Tinder match she acquired. The first principle she abided by was this: if anyone started their introductory message with a 'Hello dear' or 'Hi babe', instead of addressing her by her name, she deleted them without further thought. Another, affectionately called the castration principle, was invoked when Dani received an obscene and unsolicited photograph of a man's genitalia, which would entail a return photo of a sausage being cut in half with a pair of scissors and the words, 'Don't think I wouldn't do it.'

Strangely, this tactic worked 99 per cent of the time. But it does pose the question, why do men think sending such a photo would be a turn on for any decent woman? What am I missing here?

Dani was in her late thirties when I interviewed her, career successful, divorced for four years, two young kids under ten and in her fifth year as an expatriate. Dani was a woman who was holding life together, by managing to raise her kids alone and holding down a busy career as a corporate lawyer. All she wanted now was a decent enough man to hang out with and see where destiny took her. She had no solid expectations of what to find on Tinder, other than to filter through the undesirables to find Mr Right. She knew as well as most that there were nice guys and some not-so-nice guys out there. She just had to play the numbers game. Tinder is a pure numbers game in the sense that for every ten guys, only one might be worth meeting face to face. And even if that did happen, only one in five would be worth seeing a second time.

Nail spas offer the perfect environment to surf Tinder. Time to sit, relax, drink tea, and gently swipe away while that purple nail polish you thought was a great idea at the time, has time to dry. Dani had another principle. She would swipe on no more than twenty profiles each time she used the app. After she had reached her quota, she would stop. Having reached No. 17, it was looking like a no show for Mr Right. That is until Jack landed at No. 19. English, forties, full facial profile picture with designer stubble—yes, men do still sport the George Michael look. And to boot, he had written a few words about his passion for cycling and tennis. Dani hit the 'Super Like' icon and moved on to No. 20. Needless to say, swipe No. 20 was a left swipe given his profile picture was of him posing next to a Ferrari sports car, which most likely was not his. Even if it was, to Dani it screamed egotistical show-off. Dani obeyed her principle and closed the app.

It was a day or so later when Dani got the notification of a match with Jack, aka Mr 19. The hunt was on. Dani liked this particular moment; it was a game to see how far each encounter would go. First, the obligatory stream of messages to substantiate he lived and worked in Singapore, could spell, and hold a reasonable conversation. Next to find out if he was, in fact, single and available, and finally, if they shared common values and interests. All seemed in order after three days of messaging. Five days later, Dani stepped inside a cocktail bar, well-heeled in Louboutin, a black dress that landed just above the knee, which is the known length to be reasonable and not look too slutty. Then she proceeded to look for Jack. Having scanned a few faces, there he was, seated on a barstool not ten yards away sipping a drink.

Having approached him, 'Are you Jack?' She asked, along with a beaming smile.

'Ye, Yee, Ye, Yes.' Came the reply.

At this juncture, Dani knew, as do we all, that anyone who carries a speech impediment should not be ridiculed. It is a challenge for anyone and not an easy affliction to manage. Often the more anxious the person becomes, the more they struggle to form words. But it does require some level of understanding and acceptance on behalf of the listener. Dani offered a smile at this point and took the vacant stool next to Jack.

'So, what are we drinking?' Dani asked in the hope of relaxing her now nervous date.

'G, Gii, Gin.' Jack replied.

Dani waved to the barman and ordered a Hendricks Gin and Tonic, while secretly thinking how the evening would progress and how she would manage the situation she now found herself in.

As the G & T was being prepared, Dani knew there was only one way to approach this and that was to confront it head on. Her job as a lawyer had trained her well in how to do this. This is exactly what she did.

Dani sat upright, took one of Jack's hands gently in her own and smiled. This was followed by.

'Jack. I want you to know it's okay. Take a pause, a breath and then respond. I understand.'

Dani then took a large sip from the now much needed Gin and Tonic now resting in front of her.

'Thanks,' Jack replied in perfect form.

Dani, now more relaxed after a slug of Gin, proceeded to ask what Jack did for a career. To which Jack responded with a few stutters here and there, that he was an airline pilot. Dani, of course, wondered how he managed this form of career given his impediment. Trying not to smirk, she asked how he made the various flight announcements.

'Ca, car, carefully,' Jack replied. He too then took a sip of his drink.

'Well, at least you have a sense of humour.' She replied.

'Clearly you do,' Jack said, again in perfect diction.

At this point, Dani with her female instincts smelt a rat. Time, she decided again for a direct question.

'So, Jack. This stammer of yours . . . is it real or is this some form of silly joke?'

Jack took another sip of his drink, lent in, took Dani by the hand and replied.

'Ya, Ya, Yes. I'm just joking. I just wanted to see how you would react.'

At this point, images of herself throwing what remained of her Gin and Tonic into Jack's face seemed reasonable. But then, she could see the funny side and originality of his approach. It was a dilemma she had not faced before.

'Funny.' Is all she could muster.

Jack proceeded to explain he liked original approaches and that the last lady he had tried it on left within five minutes of meeting him. He liked to see how people reacted. Just as Dani was about to laugh it all off and not take matters further, Jack crashed and burned. There was no recovery from what he said next.

'I mean, how stupid are these women to think it's real. I'm a pilot for God's sake.'

Dani took a moment . . . held a gaze on him through her best deadpan face. It was the face she used when closing a large deal for her clients. It was her poker face.

'Actually, I did.' She retained her gaze on him.

'Really. You don't seem stupid?' Jack responded.

The Gin and Tonic Dani had been sipping found its way within seconds to Jack's smug face. Dani then got up, left, and parked the memory of having met Jack in the recesses of her mind.

The ride home in a taxi for Dani was not wasted, given it produced four more Tinder matches to consider, and the potential once again to meet Mr Right. But having met Jack, Dani now has another principle. She asks if the potential date has any afflictions she should be aware of, real or not.

SWIPE 3

Dick Pic Warrior

I must admit that I learned something new when I heard about this encounter. I tried very hard at the time to not laugh when listening. So, allow me to set some context. An exhibitionistic disorder is described in many psychological journals as being a condition marked by the urge, fantasy, or act of exposing one's genitals to non-consenting people, particularly strangers. I do hope that some of you aren't thinking, *but I do that all the time*. If you are, please get help. That said, this condition is considered a paraphilic disorder, which refers to persistent and intense atypical sexual arousal patterns that are accompanied by clinically significant distress or impairment. You get the gist I think, so let's begin.

At first sight, Jolene, at thirty-eight years of age and an American citizen, who worked as a physiotherapist in Singapore, thought the man she had just matched with had sent her a picture of a mole rat, also known as a sand puppy. Native to East Africa, the burrowing rodent is closely related to the blesmois (another mole rat, only with fur) and is the only species of the family Heterocephalidae. I'm sure you feel better for knowing that bit of natural insight. Either way, the poor old mole rat is not exactly the cutest animal on the planet, and it seemed neither was the pinkish picture of a rather wrinkly male genitalia, which now pathetically presented itself on the screen of Jolene's mobile phone.

Fortunately, Jolene had a unique way of dealing with such situations and men of this persuasion. She replied with her special message. 'I'm reporting you to the authorities for sending me the picture of a child's genitals, you sick pedophile.'

It worked every time in that she either got 'Wait! Stop. I'm not a pedophile! It's a picture of me and I'm a man.' Or, 'So sorry, it was just a joke!' Jolene never heard from them again and just to be sure, she blocked them from her account.

As the weeks passed, Jolene received a series of so-called normal matches, none of which led anywhere. Either they couldn't communicate by stringing a sentence together or couldn't spell or had some flaw in their character that sent a warning sign for Jolene to avoid them and run for the hills. One man openly declared his fetish for female feet, and another for his fancy of being spanked with a wooden spoon. Yes, all true I'm assured. Jolene also received an equal number of men who still thought it was manly to send a picture of their male junk. No message, just a picture, followed by a message asking if Jolene fancied meeting up to experience the pleasure of said man and his junk. I can hear you all sigh. But wait, there's more! Some men even went as far to name their genitalia, such as 'Little Frank', or 'Hammer head', or even 'Mini me'. And despite the annoyance of receiving such pictures, Jolene fell about laughing and duly shared the profiles and commentary with her girlfriends, so that they too could block the senders and have a good laugh at the same time. After all, why should she have all the fun, sharing is caring as they say.

It was a Sunday, and Jolene was relaxing on her couch enjoying a marathon viewing of *The Crown* on Netflix, when she received yet another visual invasion of her online decency via a picture of a man's genitalia. Only this time, Jolene studied it for a few moments. Something about it looked strangely familiar. Not that Jolene was an expert on the topic, and it certainly, was not her hobby to collect such pictures and analyse them. But a specific vein that ran down the side of the erect body part—as distinctive as the line on a subway map—drew her attention. Jolene had seen this man part before. She paused her Netflix, given looking at a man's genitals and watching the Queen of England on TV seemed at odds with each other. She now flicked through her deleted pictures and sure enough, there it was. It stood out like the Northern Line on the London Underground. This was the fourth time she had received this image but from four different profile names. Confused, but not one to give up on some fun and wanting to expose this 'Dick Pic Warrior', she fired off a message.

'Hi and wow! Fancy meeting up.' Jolene then waited for a reply, which in truth she thought she wouldn't get. Generally, the men that send these pictures have no intention of ever meeting face to face. But she was wrong. Within minutes, Sam, as was his profile name, responded with, 'Yes of course. How about Friday night?' Jolene responded with a simple 'You're on, name the time and place?'

A bar is a bar to a large degree, but Jolene had selected this one due to its propensity to have a large crowd of expats on a Friday evening. The music was blaring away, drinks by the dozen were being consumed by couples, groups of friends, work colleagues, people trying to do business and the odd single soul seated in the corner hoping to pick up someone. Jolene had dressed to kill and entered the bar dead-on 7.00 p.m. as agreed with Sam. He had indicated to her that he would be dressed in a blue shirt and jeans and sporting short, grey hair. Which, indeed, matched him perfectly as Jolene picked him out, leaning against the bar upon her arrival.

The obligatory greetings took place, and they both eased into ordering drinks and chatting away. Jolene deduced that Sam seemed normal and learned that he worked in IT as a network engineer for an insurance company. After half an hour, Jolene raised—as was her plan from the start—the elephant-in-the-room question.

'So, why send the pictures of your dick, Sam?'

This caused a moment of pause before Sam responded. 'Shock value, really. Just a joke.'

Not wanting to let him off that lightly, 'To achieve what?' She asked.

Having sipped his beer and seemingly unrattled by the direct line of questions, 'Well, you're here, aren't you? So I guess it works now and then, and I get a bit of fun for a night.'

'I see. But you have sent me your picture using many different profiles. Why?'

Sam remained cool. 'Don't think I have.'

Jolene at this juncture took a deep breath, paused, and considered her next move. It came in the form of reaching for a bell that hung above the bar, used to signal that the ringer of the bell would buy everyone in the bar a shot. Without further pause, Jolene clanged the bell as if her life depended on it, which caused an immediate roar in the bar.

Jolene was not done. She stood up and announced 'Please, Please. I need your attention everyone.' The bar fell almost silent. Sam just looked on, thinking a free drink was about to be served. Jolene continued. 'Tonight, is a special night, as I'm here with this gentleman. His name is Sam, everyone.' At this point, Sam started to wish he could vanish into the shadows for fear of being embarrassed by what he thought was a drunk Jolene. He had no idea, of course, what was to follow.

'This man is very special, because . . . wait for it everyone, he is the dick pic warrior of Tinder!'

Now before Sam's chin could hit the floor, Jolene had whipped out of her bag, glossy-printed A4 copies of Sam's genitals in all their glory and had started to hand them out to people in the bar. I'd been told the eruption in the bar was epic. People started to clap and cheer. That is except for Sam, who snatched the remaining pictures out of Jolene's hand and pushed Jolene back against the bar. Foul language was used, which was promptly halted by a six-foot two-inch giant of a man who placed a hand on Sam's shoulder and uttered in a pure Australian accent, 'Time to leave the lady alone, fella.'

Sam made a run for it and vanished as soon as his legs regained strength and his ears recovered from the rapturous laughter, aimed, of course, at him. He didn't deny it further. He didn't challenge Jolene anymore or attempt to declare her insane or hurl further abuses at her. Rather, he knew he was banged to rights and had no other option than to flee. Jolene, on the other hand, went on to be chatted up by the six-foot two-inch hunk of a single male, who had been her hero and stepped in to help her and was in the bar at the time with his rugby mates. Jolene described him as being a real gentleman. They have been going steady ever since. I guess Tinder can have a happy ending after all.

SWIPE 4

Sharing Is Not Caring

Allow me start by offering a definition of the word 'sharing'. I'm sure you are all capable of using Google, but humour me. The word is a noun. It is defined in the following words:

> The full or proper portion or part allotted or belonging to or contributed or owed by an individual or group, one of the equal fractional parts into which an item, be it food or capital stock in a bank, is divided.

Impressed? Yes, I too can use Google. But the point is we are taught from a young age to share things, given it is polite, considered caring, and a good value to have. But not everyone it seems had this value instilled in them by their role models, or perhaps they did and now have taken it too far.

The story I am about to share seems common to the online dating scene. At least, I have heard it in various forms a dozen or so times before. But this particular story is worth telling regardless. Why? Because it highlights that men in most cases, want their starter . . . in dating terms. Is this the animalistic trait most men have? We want it all, no matter what the consequences.

Dawn, forty-one-year-old attractive, natural blonde British woman, had arranged her date with Paul, having matched with him on an infamous dating app a few days before. Paul as a visual description was a well-maintained, six feet tall, handsome fifty-two year old. He dressed well, had good manners, and an easy way about him. He had divorced his wife of fifteen years, two years before. All it seemed was as normal as it could be around two people in their mid-years, who would have had certain life experiences and social baggage.

Cutting to the chase, the first date with Paul went well, in fact, extremely well. Paul, as every gentleman should, paid for drinks and some light finger food. The conversation was open, flowing, and humorous. Dawn felt at ease and the evening concluded with a respectful hug, a kiss on each cheek, and being sent home alone in a taxi. No attempt was made by Paul to try his luck with a one-night stand. Later that night Dawn replayed the date over in her head, as she showered and prepared for bed. Nothing about the date seemed to bother her, and she had decided to see him again. Just as that thought had settled in her mind, a message pinged on her phone. It was Paul. A simple message wishing her a good night and thanking her for the date and a request to see her again. Not wanting to wait, Dawn replied with a message that conveyed how much she had enjoyed his company and a second date would be most welcome. With that, she went to sleep.

Work commitments were intense over the weeks that followed, seeing Dawn sent off to Hong Kong, London, and Jakarta. That didn't seem to dull the connection between them. Almost on a daily basis messages had been exchanged, which meant to Dawn that Paul was keen, besides giving them more time to connect and share a little about their lives. Paul explained in one message exchange how his fifteen-year marriage had ended on the basis of going stale. Neither he nor his ex-wife could summon up the excitement to remain together. Their lives had simply turned into an existence, not a partnership. His two kids had grown up and left home. His wife had turned to yoga as an escape—to the extent that she spent more time in a downward-facing dog or leaping leopard posture or balanced against a wall on her head taking photos for Instagram than talking to him. Dawn found all this highly amusing and found herself liking Paul more and more. That said, Dawn was also into yoga and made a mental note not to talk about it too much with Paul or send him similar pictures of her in a yoga posture.

Some three weeks later, it was finally time was the second date. Dinner was on the cards and Paul had chosen a fine restaurant. His effort to look nice had not escaped Dawn's attention. Clean-shaven, nice shirt, and a very alluring and manly cologne that wafted across her nostrils. Paul, it seemed also appreciated the effort Dawn had made that evening, expressed in the form of the occasional hand touch, kiss on the cheek, and general petting throughout dinner. His chair had edged closer to hers with every dinner course. As Paul ordered the second bottle of wine, he had made no attempt to pretend to be a seemlier, but simply asked for a bottle of anything good. It was a point Dawn noted and liked. It showed his genuine nature and openness to be who he was and not pretend to impress.

As the evening drew to a close, which was fortunate, given Dawn could feel her dress beginning to push its limits of elasticity, she had made up her mind that she was attracted to Paul and didn't want the night to end, just yet. The stroll to the taxi queue was made hand in hand, and Dawn knew she had to make her move or wait to see if Paul would. She held her composure until a taxi drew up. Paul kissed her on the lips, the gentle kind, not I want to lasso your tonsils kind of kiss and led her to the open door of the waiting taxi.

'Fancy a coffee back at mine.' It came out of nowhere, and Dawn had even surprised herself. A moment passed.

'Love to', Paul responded and climbed in beside her. Dawn awoke about 3 a.m. and poured herself a glass of water. A broad smile had erupted across her face. It had been the best sex she had had in years, and she almost felt proud. Paul, at the time, was still in her bed, buried beneath the duvet and snoring away. One arm was hanging over the side of the bed and one of his legs jutted out at right angles.

The sun came up, they both showered, drank some coffee, kissed, and parted for their respective day jobs. A message or two was shared about the night before and Dawn was happy. It seemed she had met a man she could feel comfortable with. Saturday came around and for Dawn it meant some female pampering at the nail spa followed by drinks in the evening with two of her best friends. Paul was attending a work function with overseas visitors.

Several cocktails later, Dawn found time to have a face to face with Jane, a friend of many years and, by coincidence, also single and beginning to date. Her stories of her last date were similar to Dawn's—a real man with manners and generosity. It seemed she too had experienced incredible sex. Everything was happy until they shared pictures. Paul it seemed was getting around. They were both seeing the same man.

While Dawn and Jane came to this realization, you could argue that Paul was not doing anything wrong. Perfectly normal for a man or woman to see multiple partners if they both agree that their relationship is not exclusive. Dawn could not recall asking Paul if he was seeing anyone else, and neither could Jane. The bigger issue surfaced when Jane spoke.

'Well, no harm done, we can share, right?'

This was not something Dawn had at the top of her list and refused. So now the dilemma . . . who would tell Paul and who would step aside? Jane at that point was keen to keep seeing him.

A few days later, Paul messaged Dawn and invited her out. To which Dawn replied, 'So, you are not seeing my friend Jane that night then?'

Cool as a cucumber, Paul replied with a 'No, so I'm free.' It took an hour for Dawn to decide her next move. She simply informed Paul that she did not date men who were also seeing her friends and wished him luck. There was a boundary and friends came first. That was that.

The next time she met Jane, she asked how Paul was. They had not spoken since they've last met up. Jane replied, 'I have no idea, I changed my value system and decided that I don't share my men or date men who date my friends. There is a female code, and I now follow it.'

Friends it seems are the most precious of things and Paul it seemed had by unfortunate coincidence, obviously picked the wrong two women to date. He was never heard from again.

SWIPE 5

Being Too Nice

Why does the word 'nice' rub us up the wrong way? Why don't women want to date the nice guy? What is so wrong with nice? And, yet, doesn't every parent want their daughter to meet the nice guy?

When I researched the word 'nice', I learnt that nice used to be a negative word derived from the Latin word *nescius* meaning 'ignorant'. And, in the fourteenth century, it was used to refer to a stupid, ignorant, or foolish person. Okay, so you really didn't want to be the nice guy back then. Hey mom, here's my new stupid boyfriend . . . doesn't quite work, does it?

However, by the fifteenth century, it started to refer to a person who was finely dressed, shy or reserved, or precise. Kind of vague, but maybe nice was getting nicer? Perhaps, this is why people don't want to date the nice guy and why men don't want to be just the nice guy? Because it started out describing stupid idiots . . . great. And then it was used for generic, plain people nobody remembers . . . even better. And now, it's ended up as a synonym for 'okay' and 'obliging' (yes, I found that on thesaurus. com). So, having set the scene for this next encounter—which will enrich your experience of reading it—will demonstrate how this lady kept her cool and left the date by being the more mature person and by being . . . well, nice. But Jackie had come to the realization that nice guys aren't always what or who they seem at first.

Jackie had matched with an Asian gentleman in his early to mid-forties. A handsome enough man in that he was athletic, smooth-skinned, and well-groomed. In fact, with just the smallest of squints, you would be forgiven for thinking he was Steven Yeun, the American actor. Not just that, Alan—the name on his profile—would himself have looked perfectly at home stepping out of a trailer on a film set. At least his profile pictures indicated as much, given his elegant style of dress and naturally posed photographs in a crisp slim fit white shirt, knee-length tailored blue shorts, and Gucci loafers. It was a tick in her visual criteria box. As was the fact he had well-cut hair, no photos of him smugly hugging another woman who would later be named as just a friend, no suggestive poses trying to inflate his chest or muscles, and no poses of him behind the wheel of an expensive Italian or German sports car he had rented for the day. It was looking very positive for Jackie.

After a couple of days of exchanging messages, which further added to her attraction for Alan, it was revealed that they shared common passions—her love of art, his love of art, her love of travel, his love of travel, and he cooked too. Most important of all to Jackie, his messages were all conveyed in well-represented text messages with no grammatical errors. It concluded with them agreeing to meet. Alan selected the location and venue for the first date. Just to interject here, as I like to do from time to time, perhaps ask why do we as people put labels on things? What is a date over and above just a meet-up? I guess a date is a more romantic term and less formal and stems from the calendar reference of a particular day in a month. Anyway, a date is a date as they say.

Jackie had heard of the restaurant—it was right out of the Singapore Michelin Star Guide. She had not at that point had the chance to dine there, mainly because it took a small mortgage to do so! As such she was very excited, if not a little apprehensive knowing it was ranked so highly with two Michelin stars. It added to her viewpoint that Alan was, indeed, a man of culture and class.

Jackie arrived ten or so minutes late at the venue, an artful spot, offering an inventive, gourmet tasting menu, and ambitious cocktails with names such as 'Bloody Cologne', 'Crimson Sour', and 'Island Mist'. Its reputation as one of Asia's top 10 restaurants proceeded it. As Jackie stepped inside, it was clear why. An aroma of Moroccan figs, fresh-cut flowers, and roasting meats harmonized to lasso your senses and draw you ever further into its culinary world of splendour. How many times in her life would she experience this, she wondered? Not that her own financials would ever allow for it to become regular.

She took a seat at the bar and looked for Alan. Given he was not in view, she amused herself by people watching and wondering if they too were on Tinder dates. After five minutes or so she checked her phone to see if Alan had messaged her. He hadn't. So, Jackie switched her focus to the starched white-aproned barman taking the form of an alchemist, busy shaking, stirring, and pouring colourful cocktails. That was until a man sat down beside her, ordered a drink, and smiled at her. Cocktail after cocktail found its way to the doe-eyed couples seated around her. The man seated next to her was on his second drink, and Jackie was beginning to wonder if Alan would arrive. She fired off a message asking where he was and waited, precisely at the same time the man next to her checked his phone.

'Are you Jackie?' He asked politely.

Yes, why? What else could she reply?

'I'm Geoff, a friend of Alan's. I thought it might be you.' He turned to face her.

At this point, Jackie instinctively smelled trouble. 'What's going on here? And where is Alan?' Jackie demanded an answer.

'He can't make it and asked if I could come instead. We're friends, it's okay.'

Jackie paused a moment, with her take flight instincts now raging inside of her. 'No, this is not right. You think I'm just going to talk to a stranger? He didn't even have the courtesy to let me know.' Jackie stood up.

'I agree, and to be honest I'm not happy either. The only reason I'm here is to be a good friend and I fully understand how you feel. I apologize on behalf of both of us. And yes, you are right, I should call you a taxi and send you home.'

Jackie took a step back; it was not a response she had been expecting. It was honest and verbalized in a good tone. And clearly, the man Geoff, now seated next to her, was embarrassed given his blushing face.

'What was so important that he could not have called me himself?' Jackie wanted to understand.

'Honestly and no joke, his sister had taken ill and he just went to her as a priority, but he still wanted you to have a good night, so he called me. He can't call you because I have his phone.' Geoff playfully waved Alan's mobile phone and smiled.

Jackie at this point relaxed a little and semi-laughed. It all seemed genuine if not a little dramatic. The worst that could happen now in her view was that they continue to talk and enjoy the surreal situation. Over the next hour or so, they both continued to talk about themselves, not Alan. Geoff had divulged that he himself was single and like Jackie a member of Tinder. Hunger then got the better of both of them and not wishing to waste the opportunity to dine in style, they agreed to split the bill. They were seated at a countertop facing the kitchen, observing the chefs at work, and anxiously awaiting the five-course tasting menu with paired wines to begin.

Each course arrived along with an articulated and passionate introduction, given by the English chef. Each dish was, as Jackie recalled, a masterpiece. Unique servings of delicate fish, lamb cubes, batter dressed shrimp, green stuff, black stuff, more crispy stuff, all in a perfect artistic display, accompanied by a paired wine or cocktail.

Now all that would have been wonderful, had Geoff not developed a sudden out of body experience and become 'Mother Teresa'. He tapped Jackie gently on the shoulder and muttered, 'Is everything okay for you?' While kind of sweet the first couple of times, after twenty or thirty times, it almost sounded contrite.

Matters became worse when Geoff offered to taste everything first, just to make sure it was cooked and tasty. The final straw was when Geoff wiped the corner of Jackie's mouth with his napkin.

'Geoff, I'm not a baby,' Jackie said.

This triggered a barrage of apologies and Geoff then overkilling his humbleness and apologizing almost every minute. Even the chef rolled his eyes. As the meal progressed, he started to complain more and more, facing down the master chef and proclaiming that he expected more 'texture balance' with each dish. An all-out war had begun as the chef challenged him by reeling off how he made sure every dish was perfect—after all he was a Michelin star chef. Jackie was now having dinner with Jekyll and Hyde, on account of Geoff who had turned from Mr Nice to Mr Angry.

Thankfully for Jackie, the meal was finally over. She just wanted to leave and signalled for the cheque. As it arrived, Geoff tried to take it, a gentlemanly act, but Jackie didn't want to be in his debt. A tug of war commenced as Jackie offered her credit card, Geoff handed it back, and so it went for a minute or so. It ended with Jackie standing up and firmly pointing out she didn't want to see Geoff or Alan again. The $800 cheque was finally split between the two, and they both started to leave. But wait, Geoff insisted on ordering Jackie a taxi. Another debate ensued. Jackie then played her last card.

'Geoff, I'm going home, alone, paying my own taxi. Should you not agree, the police are just one phone call away.' She withdrew her phone and hovered a finger over the keypad. Geoff, after a moment of being in shock, walked away muttering under his breath.

On the way home, Jackie reflected on the evening and wondered how she had ended up in such a situation. The nicest of guys had turned sour, aggressive, and demanding. And, it wasn't even the man she had intended to meet!

A few days later, when Jackie's credit card statement arrived, she felt sick looking at it. Still wondering why Alan had not called to explain his part in the evening, she decided to call Alan, for no other reason than to put her mind at rest. The voice on the end of the phone was familiar in that it was Geoff—not Alan.

'Still using Alan's phone, I see.' Jackie boldly spoke.

What came next was at least honest. 'Not really, because I am Alan.'

Jackie hung up the phone, felt the wave of shock and wondered why she had not seen it before. The most bizarre of tricks had been played on her and she had been taken hook, line, and sinker. Lesson learned.

SWIPE 6

Mr Allergy

Time for a bit of medical science. I offer this snippet of information to set the scene and show that we are not all perfect, and that there may be someone who needs an extra bit of sympathy and understanding. Online dating is a big pond to fish in and you will probably encounter, mostly virtually, all kinds of people. So, here goes.

An allergy is a damaging immune response by the body to a substance, especially a particular food, pollen, fur, or dust, to which it has become hypersensitive. An allergic reaction occurs when cells in the immune system interpret a foreign substance or allergen as harmful. The immune system then overreacts to these allergens and produces histamine, which is a chemical that causes allergy symptoms such as inflammation, sneezing, and coughing.

Now, with that knowledge in mind, it's the week before New Year's Eve when Joyce had broken up with her then-boyfriend of five months. She was a little heartbroken but didn't want to let the situation bring her down. She had reminded herself at the time not to care about a guy who had cheated on her not once, but twice. The first time she had caught him while at it—doggy style, with a Vietnamese bar girl. She recalled it was much like watching two street dogs copulating! For Joyce, it was about as unpleasant an experience as she ever wanted to encounter. To make matters worse, it was *her* apartment and *her* bed on a Sunday afternoon. Having popped out for a yoga class, the last thing she expected was a sex show upon arriving home. She forgave him for no other reason than he had spoiled her with exotic vacations and jewellery. She knew it was ridiculous, but sometimes liking a guy does funny things to your brain. The second time, there was no forgiveness. She had been out for a night on the town with some girlfriends. Seeing her boyfriend with another woman leant up against a bar, with his hand openly up her short skirt was the tipping point. Had the bar not been so noisy, she swears the entire street would have heard her moans.

Fast forward to the present. Joyce loves to party, and a good year had passed since she turned single. She was seated at home drinking coffee, wondering who she could ask to chaperone her to the New Year's Eve party she had been looking forward to for months and had paid a whopping $400 for the tickets. Having exhausted her list of male friends who by now had all made plans of their own, she found herself on Tinder. This was when she met Tony—a young, charming, handsome, and dapper Englishman who promised a good time, without wanting sex. At least this was what he promised on his Tinder profile.

Joyce, during our interview, wanted to skip past the basics of how she had first met Tony online. We all know the drill. It starts with a match with someone you have liked, then an introductory exchange of messages before you agree to meet. Joyce as a point of shared fact hates messaging and had made it very clear to Tony that she only allotted a few days to ascertain if they clicked before wanting to meet face to face or move on.

Her first meeting with Tony was unlike a typical Tinder date. She had decided a walk in the Botanical Gardens would suffice and would give them both the opportunity to meet and talk without noise, alcohol, and other similar distractions. The sun was out, the humidity was tolerable, and all seemed well. Tony's first scratch came about fifteen minutes after they had met at the main gates, the second flurry of scratches at his arms and chest, not long after that. Entering the orchid gardens it seemed had set off some bodily chain reaction in Tony's physiology, and he was starting to look rather red. Joyce, of course, enquired about his well-being. This is where she discovered Tony had an allergy to pollen and all things plant-based.

Later, in the protective sanctum of an air-conditioned café some miles away from the Botanical Gardens, coffee and carrot cake had arrived. What else to do but enjoy and tuck in. That was the moment when the drama started to unfold.

It is now well-established that nut allergy is one of the most common allergies in children and although in most cases the severity of the allergy diminishes as they grow older, there are some for whom, it gets worse. Yes, you guessed it, Tony had not overcome this problem—in particular, his allergy to walnuts, which were part of the carrot cake topping.

Symptoms of a nut allergy vary and range from milder reactions to a severe allergic reaction called anaphylaxis. The most common symptom of a nut allergy is raised red bumps of skin, commonly known as hives, though other allergic symptoms such as a runny nose, cramps, nausea or vomiting can also surface. Obvious to most, the best way to manage an allergy to nuts is to avoid all products containing these foods. So why did Tony not take this precaution but instead continued to eat the walnuts? Joyce had no idea, given she had no idea Tony had such an allergy as she started to observe Tony morphing into something you would see on Halloween night. His eyes started to swell up first, then bumps appeared all over his skin. The situation got worse when his breathing started to get very shallow. Joyce was not in any way medically trained, but she knew enough to know that food allergies can be life-threatening. Tony was having a severe allergic reaction. She had no choice and called for an ambulance.

It's a strange thing seeing someone you don't really know being carted off to the hospital. But out of conscience, guilt, and maybe even a tinge of embarrassment and shame she had decided to go with him to the hospital. It was the decent thing to do after all.

Naturally, Joyce had no answers to the many questions she was asked by the hospital staff about his medical history. Joyce had tried to make clear that she had only just met him and was not his wife. Perhaps she should have just said he was a Tinder date and left it at that. In most probability, half the hospital staff were also on the same site. That aside, she did share his earlier reaction to the orchids and the fact they had eaten carrot cake.

Having been given a shot of adrenaline, Tony started to recover a few hours later. It is fair to say that their first date had not gone as expected.

A week or so later, Tony messaged Joyce—not called—messaged and apologized. He wanted to make it up to her. Joyce by this time had started to see another man, but given it was very early stages, she agreed to meet Tony for a drink. At least they could share a laugh about what had happened, and no lasting harm had been done. The perfect cocktail bar was the venue of choice and they both settled down to talk about the unfortunate events of their first date. At least Tony could laugh about it and swore he would be more careful in the future. Tony was charming and humorous, and Joyce found herself liking him. She sipped her Whiskey Sour while Tony enjoyed his Irish whiskey. Or, so it seemed at the beginning. For the uninitiated, Irish whiskey is not what one would think of when considering yeast-free alcohol. But, believe it or not, this beverage is made with only three ingredients—malted barley, unmalted barley, and pure water. And so, it began. Itchy mouth, eyes, and nose. Hives, itchiness on his skin, and swelling of his face followed by wheezing and difficulty breathing. Tony was encountering another allergic reaction to the barley in his cocktail! Joyce, and realizing by now that she needed an ambulance on speed-dial, called for help. Tony was again taken away. Joyce avoided the opportunity to play Florence Nightingale and went home instead. A few hours later Joyce did call the hospital to make sure Tony was okay, but that was the last time she contacted him. Sometimes, enough is enough, and Joyce concluded that Tony should either date a doctor or nurse and she would avoid becoming one.

SWIPE 7

Odour Most Foul

There is one thing we all find either acceptable or in extreme cases, highly offensive. That thing in the context of this encounter is body odour. Yes, that unseen phenomenon that finds its way up your nostrils and makes you want to vomit. To be scientific for a moment; it is present in all animals and humans, and its intensity can be influenced by many factors—stress, exercise, medical conditions, and levels of poor hygiene. In most cases, body odour has a strong smell and is considered by most cultures as offensive. That said, in some cultures, it is considered a sign of masculinity. For our next lady, you could argue she got exactly that upon her first meet.

Kim, by way of introduction is a Singaporean-American mix lady, well-educated, well-dressed, good job, and a nine on the attractiveness scale. She also smelt gorgeous on account of Chanel. And, in her own words, she was not a lady in need of repair.

One Saturday evening, she had walked right into a wall of masculine odour most foul when she met David for the first time. The odour was so foul, in fact, it would make a rotting fish smell like the sweat of an angel. Her initial reaction was to recoil having been embraced by him in an over-familiar bear hug within moments of her meeting him, followed by dropping herself onto a barstool and putting her fingers to her nose as inconspicuously as she could. Kim then composed herself as David looked on and took a seat beside her. The date had not started well. David proceeded to order drinks and act as if nothing was wrong. Perhaps, in his mind, nothing was wrong as he started to chat about his delight in meeting her.

David was of mixed origin too, and best described as Eurasian. Average build, mid-forties, and worked in the insurance industry. The conversation, as it had begun over messenger before they had agreed to meet, was comfortable and Kim had felt at ease. But the smell kept pushing its way up her nostrils with every movement of David's body. It was so pungent, in fact, that the couple seated next to them had moved to the far end of the bar. Not even the sweet smell of the Gin she had ordered would dull her senses.

'Hard day at work, was it?' Kim had to ask.

'Not particularly, no,' David responded.

Kim now had to find another way to alert David to his state of hygiene and wanted to avoid being rude or causing offense. She made excuses and went to the restroom, pushing herself through the throng of people. As she powdered her nose, she first thought was to leave, or just simply tell him about his odour. But Kim was not one to be that bold. David seemed nice; so, she considered it would be a shame to end the date if he had a reasonable excuse for his condition.

On her way back to him, she passed a single man seated at a small table. He was quietly enjoying a bottle of beer and minding his own business. Kim stopped and said hello. The man offered a hand and introduced himself as Ken, a native Australian.

'Would you consider helping me out?' Kim asked.

'Sure love, what's the problem?' Ken seemed amenable to help.

'My date tonight. I just met him. Well, he has an odour problem and I have no idea how to tell him without causing offense.'

Ken didn't take long to understand. 'So, you want me to tell him?'

'Would you mind, but make it not obvious I have asked?' She smiled.

'Sure, no worries, where is he?' Ken put down his beer and followed Kim.

As Kim took her seat next to David, Ken hovered in the background. He then made his approach.

'Sorry to disturb you nice folks, but fella, you need a shower. Else this lovely lady will be on her toes.' Ken delivered the message and winked at Kim before strolling back to his place at the bar. Now to picture this, Ken was about four inches taller and wider than David, so David slackened his jaw, looked somewhat shocked, closed his mouth again and turned to Kim.

'Do I smell that bad?' He sniffed himself.

Kim had no choice now. 'I'm afraid so. I didn't want to say anything.' She smiled.

David sniffed himself again.

'I'm so sorry. I didn't realize.'

Confession is the best medicine, and Kim liked the fact David had apologized. The evening continued, with Kim not getting too close and they agreed to meet again for lunch the next day. David agreed to check his deodorant and apply it should he need to.

It was Sunday, a day edged with blue skies and filled with the warm balmy tropical heat of Singapore. For many, it was also a popular day for chilling out and long brunches with friends. But for Kim, it would turn out to be a Sunday she wished she had stayed at home. David had been invited at the last minute to join Kim and a selection of her friends for brunch. She had forgotten the arrangement and decided not to call it off with David and combine the appointments. The hotel hosting the brunch, the Grand Hyatt, put on a champagne brunch worthy of kings, and it was not something to miss. Wearing a light flowing cotton white dress, Chanel scent, semi-sensible wedge shoes, just high enough to make her feel sexy, Kim arrived and took her seat at the round table set for ten. Two of her closest friends, Carol and Jean had already arrived. The champagne had already begun to flow.

It was some thirty minutes later that David arrived, looking sheepish, as he joined the table now filled with females and two other males. He took his seat next to Kim and introduced himself. Eyes rolled as he did so, and Kim looked on in horror. David had yet again arrived and with him an odour most foul. Chairs began to shuffle away from him as Kim stood up and asked David to join her for a short walk.

'David—is there a problem I should know about. You stink.' Kim could not contain her embarrassment or anger this time.

'Sorry, I didn't have time to shower after my run.'

Kim paused for a moment.

'Please leave. I can't imagine how you could ever arrive at a lunch knowing you have body odour problem! It's so embarrassing.'

Kim departed and rejoined her friends.

As for David, he left, no doubt for home, a shower, and a visit to a pharmacy for some high-powered deodorant.

The moral of this story—and yes, it did happen—is don't go on a date with BO. It's not cool, and you just end up looking like a dick, or worse, smelling like a dead cat.

SWIPE 8

Fashion Victim

Fashion is a strange thing if one can even call it a 'thing'. Perhaps 'phenomenon' is a better-suited word. An all-encompassing definition of fashion would take up an entire book, but briefly it can be said to be a popular style of clothing, hair, decoration, or behaviour. Fashion has for sure been through many adaptations over the years. It would be fair to say that we each have our own preferences for what fashion we embrace, like or dislike. But we also have certain expectations of what is tasteful, classic or in contrast, outrageous. I recall my father falling backwards in shock when I arrived home one day with a skinhead haircut and a pair of Doctor Martin boots. 'It's just fashion, dad', I recall saying. Not that it stopped me from getting a good lecture on decency and how to dress. My parents you see were highly conservative and had invested their hard-earned cash on my public school education. As such, I was expected to wear sweaters and blazers. My point here is that sometimes our personal upbringing can dictate how we present ourselves.

Emma, a British and forty-three-year-old business consultant, could be described as a classic dresser. The appropriate little black dress for evenings, a white blouse with jeans on a casual Friday, shorts and a t-shirt when pushing the shopping cart around the supermarket on a weekend. The florescent green spandex she wears when inducing a sweat at the gym is probably a little out of character, but hey . . . none of us are perfect! The fact is, nothing about Emma's fashion choices could be labelled as offensive.

Emma was also a lady of tradition. When going on a first date, she would make every effort to look well-maintained by putting her best-pedicured foot forward, hair groomed, fingernails polished, breath fresh, and present as best she could a visual feast for the man she was about to meet. Never did she ever look like a street hooker or a woman who had lost the will to live. Let's face it, men and women all shop with their eyes first, right? As it is said, first impressions count.

Emma was approaching her twelve-month anniversary as a Tinder user. During this period, she believed she had met or chatted with every weirdo on the planet. Ranging from men who wanted one-night stands to men with strange fetishes, along with the married ones and the off-shore business traveller in need of a weekend date. She considered herself by this time a seasoned user of the site and could easily spot a good egg from a bad one. The last Tinder date she had encountered would certainly not be awarded the good egg prize. A visiting British male, Kevin, who believed he could influence Emma to have a one-night stand on account of him being misunderstood by his wife. Yes, that was the actual reasoning he used to justify his request. Emma had unfortunately accepted a drink with him prior to knowing this, so found herself in need of an exit strategy when the proposition came. The 'phone a friend' trick was used during a restroom break, and within minutes of her returning to the table, her phone rang. It was Sally, a close friend, asking her to return home urgently as her apartment had flooded. What would we do without friends? Emma left and that was that.

After a week or so, David, her next Tinder date, was an Australian. In his forties, physically in good shape and with a good sense of humour—or so it seemed from his messages. His profile picture presented his manly self on a beach in a wetsuit clutching a surfboard. Emma was perfectly happy with this first impression. Emma had displayed a profile picture of herself sitting at a desk, dressed respectfully for work. All good so far. After a few days of getting to know each other in basic form, and to eliminate the chances of either one of them being fake or armed with the wrong intentions, they both decided to throw caution to the wind and agreed to meet over dinner at a restaurant known for its Michelin stars. Emma shared with me that this would not have been her primary choice given it was a first date, and she was not expecting anything other than a casual drink to break the ice in person. Liking someone over messaging and liking them in person is very different. The only way to test the chemistry is to meet the person nose to nose. Despite Emma suggesting a more casual date, David had insisted on dinner, and the romantic gesture had not gone unnoticed. What woman would not like to be treated like a queen and the promise of a great meal, fine wine, and good conversation? Chivalry and romance it seemed were not dead.

Emma arrived fifteen minutes late, for no other reason than traffic was heavy and walking the 450 metres from the taxi drop off to the restaurant inside the world-renowned Marina Bay Sands complex in Singapore, on the polished marble floors, in her five-inch heels, took a little more effort. But arrive she did.

Meanwhile, David was comfortably seated at a table for two, to which Emma was shown by the restaurant concierge.

Upon her arrival, David stood up and greeted her with a gentle embrace and a kiss on the cheek. At this point, Emma drew in a sharp breath. David stood before her dressed in a mould-stained and deplorable old singlet, which marketed some form of Thai beer, faded board shorts, bottomed off with a pair of well-worn thongs. Yes, it was the traditional Aussie-man attire many believe Australians wear, and David had proven the point that it was not a myth. While this may be fine as an outfit to wear on weekends while watching the footy with your mates—and one could say typical of the laid-back Australian view on life—but for a first date in a Michelin star restaurant, Emma could be forgiven for viewing this as no effort having been made whatsoever.

Having seated herself, Emma waited to be offered a drink. Could things get worse, she wondered? It did. David sipped his beer and offered her the same. At that point, Emma simply stated she preferred wine, which was immediately challenged on the basis that David had browsed the menu and deduced it was far too expensive. Emma, having noted the second disappointment, said that she would cover the cost and proceeded to order a bottle of French red.

As they both settled in and ordered the main meal, a choice of prime rib steak for him and grilled salmon and sides for Emma, she couldn't help but notice Dave's sharp intakes of breath. Asking if there was a problem, David announced he hoped they were going Dutch as he couldn't justify the expense. This is the point where the world stopped spinning, and Emma needed to speak her mind.

'Can I ask why you agreed to meet me here, David? I would have been just as happy with a drink in a bar. And perhaps your dress code would have been more appropriate.'

What followed was a reply that made Emma drain of blood. His response was along the lines of, 'I never pay on the first date love, just in case we don't click.'

Emma considered her next move and took a sip of wine. It played out in her mind first. She would request the bill, pay her half, and offer him some constructive advice. Something along the lines of, when inviting a lady to dinner, either pay or make it clear up front that it was your preference to share the cost of the dinner. And given this, do not insist on the venue until you have done so. Second, dress to impress. If she had wanted to date a beach bum, she could have found one on Bondi beach. And besides, should she be in need of public embarrassment—evident by the rolling of eyes each waiter and customer had given them since she arrived—by taking a slob to dinner, she would have done so in the mindset of being on a comedy reality show. She drew a deep breath and delivered the message, just as she had rehearsed it in her mind. David took it in, watched her pay the bill and stood up. He looked at her for a moment and walked away. With that Emma shouted, 'And where do you think you are going, I only settled my bill, not yours.' The restaurant went silent and Emma felt everyone staring at her.

David turned to leave. 'Please, stop him.' She shouted at no one in particular. As is normal in such situations, everyone pretended not to hear and chose not to become involved. That is aside from the head waiter who stepped in front of David and gestured for him to return to the table. 'Mate, you need to move out the way.' David passed him by and left.

The evening concluded with Emma trying to explain for a half-hour to the restaurant's management what had transpired and asking them for David's details. In her opinion, they must have had at least his mobile number when the reservation was made. They did indeed have it, but the two calls made to him went unanswered. Emma was left with two choices, call the Police and ask for help, or pay and leave. She chose the second option and never logged into Tinder again, except for deleting her profile for good.

SWIPE 9

The Science of Love

Science has identified three basic parts of love, each driven by a unique cocktail of brain chemicals. Lust is governed by both oestrogen and testosterone, in both men and women. Attraction is driven by adrenaline, dopamine, and serotonin—the same chemicals that are released when reading an exciting novel, just like this one! Well, I had to try, right? But jokes apart, although love has long been a subject for consideration among philosophers and poets, there is an actual science to love. Being in love is affected by huge, measurable changes in the biochemistry of the brain. Long-term attachment is governed by a very different set of hormones and brain chemicals—oxytocin and vasopressin, which encourage bonding. I said bonding, not bondage. That topic requires an entirely different mix of chemicals, mainly alcohol and illegal substances. Moving on, interestingly, oxytocin is known as the cuddle hormone and is the hormone that drives the bond between mother and child. Each of these chemicals works in a specific part of the brain to influence lust, attraction, and attachment.

Science has also shown that the process of falling in love can, in some cases, be hurried along. In a small-scale study, subjects who talked deeply to a perfect stranger for thirty minutes, and then stared into each other's eyes for four minutes, felt a deep and lasting attachment. One pair even went on to marry! So, there you have it, try it!

Claire, having read an article on the science of love in a female glossy one Saturday afternoon, decided to put it into practice. Her next task while sitting under the hairdryer was to start swiping on possible males upon whom she could run her test.

The first few swipes were a slam dunk left swipe, meaning reject. Okay, I can hear you asking why? Well, I was informed by Claire that any man posing with someone that clearly has pole dancing on their resume was a complete no-no. The same with a profile showing a bowl of fruit with a banana as the focal point, as any profile with no picture at all. So, on she went. A few right swipes were made—twenty-two, in fact, before she was taken out from under the hairdryer and pampered for the next fifteen minutes with a shoulder rub. So relaxing was the treatment, Claire had to postpone her swiping until later.

Later, at home with a cup of Earl Grey tea in one hand and her iPhone in the other, Claire was back at it, swiping away in Tinder, when Boom! a match came in with a loud *Ping*. He was lucky No. 38. A trio of imaginary trumpets sounded off in her head and Claire went on to read his profile. Ben, forty-two, English, working as a marketing executive. He went on to proclaim his love of cinema, coffee, and treks in the mountains. Oh, and let's not forget he also claimed to be a down-to-earth guy. Now, for the point of discussion, I was once told by a female friend, that saying that you are a down-to-earth guy is read by some women as boring. Well, true or not, Claire had not heard about that view and fired off a message.

Ben responded within the hour with a polite, 'Nice to connect.' Followed by, 'If you were a superhero, which one would you choose.' Somewhat an original question but also a little cheesy at the same time. At least, he didn't ask what her job was—also a no-no as a first question for Claire.

Claire decided to play along and responded with 'Captain Marvel'. Of course, she had to ask Ben the same question. His response was even blander than hers, 'Iron Man'. Yes, Claire did yawn for a second. The conversation went on and all seemed well. Ben had been polite, humorous, and responsive. Claire could tick off a few boxes. Then it was action time, the invite came to meet up, which Claire deliberately took an hour or so to respond to. Something along the lines of treat them mean to keep them keen.

Anyway, she accepted. Date, time, and place were agreed on. But not before Claire did some more research on her now favourite field of study—the science of love.

She read that scientists in fields ranging from anthropology to neuroscience have been asking this same question—albeit less eloquently—for decades. It turns out that the science behind love is both simpler and more complex than we might think. When Claire Googled the phrase 'biology of love', she got answers that run the gamut of accuracy. Needless to say, the scientific basis of love is often sensationalized, and as with most science, we don't know enough to draw firm conclusions about every piece of the puzzle. What she did discover, however, is that much of love *can* be explained by chemistry. So, if there's really a 'formula' for love, what is it, and what does it mean? She continued her research.

Think of the last time you ran into someone you find attractive. You may have stammered, your palms may have sweated, or you may have said something incredibly asinine and tripped spectacularly while trying to saunter away (or, is that just me?). And chances are, your heart was thudding in your chest. It's no surprise that, for centuries, people thought love—and for that matter, most other emotions— arose from the heart. As it turns out, love is all about the brain—which, in turn, makes the rest of your body go haywire.

The evening had arrived, and Claire made every effort to dress well. Not too sexy and not too plain. Heels under five inches, a plain black tight-fitting dress and a simple necklace, topped off with her favourite Tom Ford scent named 'Rose Prick'. Her mission was to arouse the testosterone levels in Ben within moments of meeting him. Claire stressed at this point of telling me her story that she wanted to stimulate attraction, not, she added firmly, to invite a one-night stand. To her delight, Ben arrived bang on time and presented himself in a classic blue suit with an open-neck white shirt. The chemistry had started to fizz. A gentle hug, followed by a kiss on the cheek, and Claire stared directly into Ben's eyes. Would it work, she wondered, as she started to unleash her 'weapons' of love.

The occasional touch of Ben's arm, looking more into his eyes, and leaning towards him were all played out. Ben seemed to be responding with similar acts, and his smile beamed. That was until Claire began to ask herself if she was leading him on a little, rather than letting nature take its course and decided to focus more on just talking. The words 'be careful what you wish for' flashed through her mind. 'So, Ben. Tell me about you?' Ben responded happily. Nothing too wild, other than his separation from his wife of eight years, no kids, loving his job, having just won a deal to market a new online shopping platform, and he had two brothers. Ben seemed every bit a regular guy. That is until he asked, 'So, you are aware you have been flirting with me, aren't you?' Claire sat back and replied with 'Was I?' Knowing fully well that she had been caught in the act, and Ben it seemed was not so normal but very attuned to reading people. He further demonstrated by stating, 'I have to read people in my line of work, marketing is about knowing people.' He smiled.

A thought crossed Claire's head. Should she confess? She decided there was nothing to lose and went on to explain to Ben that she had been researching, with good intent, the science of love, for no other reason but to enhance her chances of finding her Mr Right. Ben listened intently as they both consumed a bottle of wine and laughed along the way. Ben was fascinated, and the conversation kept them talking for two hours. In reality, it had been the perfect evening. At the stroke of midnight, given it was a weekday, Ben politely paid the bill and put Claire on a taxi home. He had been the perfect gentleman.

As Claire jumped into bed, alone, she wondered if her honesty had struck a chord with Ben. He seemed interested in the subject of conversation, and she definitely hoped to see him again. But as the days passed, she began to think he had run for the hills. Two of her messages had no replies. She decided to focus on two other matches she had received on Tinder. The first was of medium interest given he had very young children and by admission was going through a bitter divorce. He got points for his honesty. The second match, a Dutchman, seemed to have a problem spelling properly and was subsequently dropped from further communication.

Just as Claire was about to start swiping, a message from Ben appeared on her phone. He had been travelling and having now returned wanted to meet up. Claire could not help but smile and immediately accepted the invitation. This was followed by her promise of no more flirting. The date was set for a Saturday evening for drinks and some good conversation. Ben again arrived on time and Claire felt the chemistry immediately. Ben, however, seemed a little more chilled out. 'Have you ever considered what you want in a man?' He asked.

Claire took a moment and considered her response. 'Yes. Honesty and loyalty above all else.' She replied.

Ben considered, 'What about passion in the physical sense—important or not?'

'Of course, important.' Claire felt herself blush. At this point, Ben sat back and shared his views on lust.

In summary, he stated that lust is driven by the desire for sexual gratification. The evolutionary basis for this stems from our desire to reproduce—a need shared by all living things. Claire listened and felt a little like a student in a biology class. The insight continued until Claire felt the need to change the topic.

'So, how was your business travel?' She enquired.

'Good, but you have made an assumption about me, and I need to confess something.' Ben looked rather serious.

'Oh God, you're still married, aren't you?' She asked.

'No, my divorce is real. But we haven't talked about the reason.' He stated.

By this time, Claire just wanted to get to the point, given Ben clearly had some terrible confession to make. 'So, tell me?' She prepared for the worse.

'I'm dysfunctional in the male genitals and can't get an erection.' Ben came out with it.

Claire regretted her next comment as it blurted out of her mouth, 'Oh my God.' Which was bad enough, but the laugh that followed really didn't help.

'So, you see, for all of your interest in the science of love, the physical aspect which you have just stated as important, can't happen.' With that Ben paid and left.

On the way home, Claire felt somewhat ashamed. Should she not have laughed? Should she maybe have said that there are other ways to pleasure each other. But it was all a little late. Ben was gone, and she never received a reply to her apology message and the request to meet again.

In the end, Claire did indeed learn much about the science of love—in that laughing at a man's dysfunctional afflictions did nothing to stimulate chemicals in the brain, other than to walk away. Claire was more careful by her own admission to not ever do it again. Her Tinder dates continue.

SWIPE 10

The American Somalian

This is a sad story, and it is Tina's story. When she shared it with me, I was not horrified as I had heard of other such stories before. But I was surprised given Tina appeared to be an intelligent lady and also seemed to be very streetwise. This story shows just how easily a genuine and intelligent person can be deceived and parted from their hard-earned cash. It is a known fact that millions of people turn to online dating apps or social networking sites to meet potential partners. I have and I suspect you have too. But instead of finding romance, so many of us have found a scammer hiding behind what seemed like a genuine profile. The objective of such scammers is simple—they try to trick trusting people into sending them money. In 2019, a staggering $201 million exchanged hands as a result of romance scams. What is even more disturbing is that people reported losing more money to romance scams in the past two years than any other form of fraud.

The modus operandi of many romance scammers is to bait the hook for you to bite. These people typically create fake profiles on dating sites and apps or contact their targets through other popular social media sites such as Instagram, Facebook, or Google Hangouts. The scammers take their time to build a relationship with their potential victims by asking personal questions—all aimed at getting to know their lifestyles and other important pieces of information such as occupation, age, hobbies, family background, and so on. Don't be fooled, they are profiling you. It's worth researching this subject to protect yourselves. Something Tina wished she had done.

Having matched on Tinder, the man introduced himself to Tina as John Hodges, supposedly an engineer from Houston, Texas. His profile picture was very American, a middle-aged man, sporting socks with sports shoes, knee-length shorts, and a plaid check shirt. His grey hair made him look older than his fifty years. But to Tina, a woman in her fifties, he was perfect. Mature, solid, and not overly flashy. They spent several weeks sharing text messages, phone calls, and emails, but never actually meeting face to face, not even on video. Tina had requested to Skype, but various excuses were given, ranging from he could not use his work computer for such things to his Skype account that encountered issues. Despite these evasions, Tina continued to trust him.

Tina confided in me that the conversation started to get pretty intense fairly quickly.

'I love you; I want to be with you for the rest of my life.' Came one message, with lots of passion and lots of attention.

'You are starting to make me feel very special.' Came another. Tina was beginning to fall for John as she too had been devoid of love and attention for some years. John had discovered her weakness—Tina craved and wanted attention. But within a few weeks, those declarations of love and romantic gestures were interspersed with requests for money. The scam had begun.

The problem was Tina had not realized it yet. John had informed Tina that he was in a financial fix due to his former wife withdrawing money from an account he used for travel expenses. He needed to travel to Egypt on business and had to pay for the trip himself before he could claim expenses. This, John added, was company policy. If he could not do this, his company would fire him. Seems extreme, right? But Tina had become blinded by her romance with John and common sense had eluded her on this occasion. John needed $5,000 to cover his airfare and hotel expenses. Tina had fallen for it and wired the funds to a very appreciative John. In return, he promised to return the funds the moment his expenses were cleared by the company. A few weeks passed with John messaging before the next request landed. It was one catastrophe after the next and his excuses were beginning to become excessive. His excuses ranged from, he had lost his tools and needed money to rent them to he needed funds to pay customs officials. Tina recalls now with a clear head 'That it was as if I knew something was coming, but you're in so, so deep you just play it through,' Tina said. Over the course of a month, she recalls having sent John over $25,000.

It was one Saturday afternoon when Tina felt something was very wrong, given no sign of John's expenses being paid and this in turn being sent back to her. Her requests to know the status of the payment had been fobbed off with excuses. She decided to meet John, even if it meant her flying to see him in Houston. John agreed to meet her a week later. Tina had some vacation time and booked her flight. Yes, this is the extremes the hopelessly infatuated or hopelessly in love will go to. Of no surprise, John cancelled the meeting a day before Tina was due to fly, given he had been asked by his company to visit the UK to land a big construction job. Four months and thousands of dollars later, Tina had had enough and told John she couldn't give him any more money.

'I had sent this man a total of almost $50,000 by this time.' She recalls.

It ends with John deleting his profile and Tina having never seen a dime returned. And after logging a police report, Tina learnt that she had most likely lost her money for good. The chances of finding the man behind the name John she was told was rare, and he was clearly a scam artist. The email and phone numbers he had used were also fake but had been tracked back to a Somalian man who was known to be part of a network of scam artists, who yes, all claimed to be from Houston. The bank accounts given had been closed long ago. Tina had learned a painful and costly lesson. Her hope is that all women learn from this and do not fall for the same or similar scams while trying to find the near-perfect, even normal *safe* man.

Unfortunately, stories like Tina's are not rare at all. I have read many articles recently about online dating scams—the same basic story only with slightly different details: victim enrols in an online dating site; meets a man with whom she exchanges frequent phone calls and online chats, although they actually never meet face to face; the man claims to be in love and then starts sharing sad stories which can only be alleviated if the woman sends money.

A couple of months after I had listened to Tina's encounters, another lady came forward and shared that she too had had frequently crossed paths with would-be scammers. Her description of a generic love-scammer sounded almost exactly like 'John Hodges' from Houston, Texas. They *all* seem to be . . . engineers, alone in the world, waiting for a huge cheque from someone. The biggest tipoff is when you ask them where they live. In most cases, it is the US.

Engineer? Check. Single? Of course. Currently in the US (and thus conveniently unavailable for face-to-face meetups). Ditto. Waiting for a huge check? Well, John's requests for loans to pay for alleged business trips or manage company payroll, sort of falls into that category.

The best way to protect yourself from such scams is to remember that in most cases you would probably not give money to people you *know*, let alone some stranger. You cannot fall in love with a photo in a profile—you need to see the *real* person. Which is just another way of saying: If you've never been in the same room with a person, you don't know them well enough to trust them with your money!

SWIPE 11

The Serial Swiper

This is Phoebe's story. It's the personal account of a date she had with a man called Scott. It's a story told so well by her, I will write it exactly as she told me. No embellishments added to bring it to life and no polish to make it sparkle. Just the raw words as they passed from her lips and into my ears. To not write it in this way, would simply not do her story justice. And, so she began.

It was a Sunday afternoon as I recall. We were seated in a café. Two coffees, my laptop open. I had swiped right on 200 desperate-looking male profiles before I matched with Scott. Just a week later, I had started to date him face to face. He was a little chubby, kind of like a small silver back Gorilla in a suit, but he had presence and possessed certain other skills that I liked.

'The world is in a bloody mess, and I think it will collapse. Bloody virus!' Scott boomed as if to the entire restaurant. His face was flushed pink, like a fresh salmon as I remember. Over-indulged on red wine, I thought.

Normally, I'm Phoebe the calm, the patient, the mild-mannered, the reliable, and the logical. But I swear that after just ten minutes in the company of Scott on this particular evening, I contemplated changing my principles. Yes, the deadly Covid-19 virus had affected us all, but life must go on I thought. Although I did wonder why I hadn't used it as an excuse not to go out that evening with Scott. Had I done so, I would not have been sitting there. I was sorely tempted to jab him in the foot with one of my pointy heels, which at the time were pinching me and making me all the more uncomfortable. I wondered if by doing so it would deflate his pompous and self-righteous ego, and he would fly off like a burst balloon.

Trust me, I do not normally possess homicidal maniac tendencies, but the thought of deflation by stabbing him was a nice fantasy . . . can you imagine the look on his face if I had. Not to mention if he had exploded like a lanced boil all over the restaurant—what a mess!

Scott at that point took hold of my free hand and gave it a squeeze and cast his charming smile at me. His smile was the reason I swiped on him in the first place. That, and as I discovered later, he was amazing in the bedroom—and by that, I mean earthquake good! I slipped off my painful heels under the table and smiled back, more from the relief that my feet had been liberated and blood circulation had returned than on account of Scott earning it. But he didn't know that.

Scott's smile grew bigger, and I knew what it meant and that was, he would come by later, meaning Scott would stay over at my apartment—something he liked to do on Friday nights. But first, we had to finish dinner.

It was almost midnight by the time we reached my home, but Scott performed as expected, and he and I were both satisfied. But the next morning, I felt differently. I had come to the realization that Scott was not a keeper, and I needed to try someone new. I simply told him that I was bored of him, and not even his bedroom talents were sufficient to keep my interest. He dressed and as he reached the front door I told him it was over. I didn't want to continue seeing him. He left along with his inflated ego and that was that.

I was over him in about ten minutes. That's how long it took for him to leave my apartment and for me to fire up Tinder.

Lee, a British, thirty-year-old man who looked somewhat like a poked weasel, which for those of you who don't know what a weasel is, it's a small slender carnivorous mammal related to, but smaller than a stoat. Now imagine poking such an animal with a stick. It would turn, bare its teeth and looked somewhat annoyed. This is what Lee reminded me of. Why he appealed to me in the first place still puzzles me, but hey, any port in a storm. We matched, and it all started again. We messaged, flirted, dated, and became intimate. That was until after a week I was bored of him too. I had come to my senses, given friends had also thought that he looked like a weasel. So, I sent him on his way too.

By now my finger was fighting fit for swiping and I matched with Tony, a forty-year-old Brit. At this point I will skip over the merry dance of messaging, and we arrived at dinner for our first date. Tony would struggle to hold a conversation with his mother let alone me. So, I glanced furtively around the restaurant and froze midway as I locked eyes with a man at the next table. As soon as he realizes I've caught him, he looks back to his companion—his exquisite blond companion, I must emphasize.

Now this guy was to-die-for gorgeous, the kind of guy you would crawl across broken glass for, naked, just to touch his knees. He was dangerous handsome. The kind of handsome women line up just to get their hearts broken. Although I am not immune to a bit of male flattery, I just didn't get why he kept staring at me. This, even the more surprising, since he was seated across a woman that would pass as a supermodel.

By now Tony had realized I was distracted and drew my attention back to him. We chatted for a bit, but I just wasn't into him. To be honest, chatting to a dead fox on the road would have been more interesting. So, I clammed up and focused fully on the desert course that had just arrived in front of me, before I opened my big mouth and said something to upset him. Meaning I actually *wanted* to tell him right there and then that he was boring, and if I were seated in front of a catholic priest hearing my confession, I would probably be having more fun!

'Oh, awesome! Chocolate mousse. I love chocolate mousse . . . all that lovely mouth-watering silk that melts in your mouth!'

'Am I boring you?' Tony asked me.

'Don't be silly!' I replied as devoured another spoonful of chocolate heaven. Tony then repeated his question quietly. Resisting the urge to flick a spoonful of mousse at him to break the tension, I lied. I tell him no, how could he possibly think such a thing. But it didn't wash of course as I looked away to lock eyes again with the handsome hunk on the next table—who, again, was looking right back at me!

At this point, Tony stood up and walked away, I assumed for a smoke or a bio break. But he never returned, and I ended up paying for dinner. The handsome hunk left too with his blonde stick of a woman, but not before sending me a wink. He was a definite ship that passed in the night.

The next morning, I set off for work. The taxi route was much the same, and I had little to think about . . . certainly not

Tony. Even the handsome man had faded given I don't like what I can't have. So yes, I did look at Tinder and promised myself this would be the last time I used it—much like an alcoholic makes a promise not to drink anymore.

What can I say, it becomes habitual and I was an addict. As my daily shot of Tinder coursed through my veins, I was swiping far too many times left. Not a single profile hit me like a lightning bolt. Needless to say, the profiles with food as their image or a landscape were passed by without a nanosecond of thought. That was, of course, until Jeremy popped up. He was Australian, thirties, and average looking. He had also bothered to write three lines about himself. The swipe right was made and *strike*, we matched! I was a Tinder alcoholic and I had just found a bottle of vodka.

The first date went well. Jeremy was charming, and we had good conversation. We connected on a number of levels. He loved art, I loved art. He loved keeping fit, I sort of kept fit. He liked to cook, and I too loved to cook. Even our taste in weird eclectic music and film genre were aligned.

The second date, we moved a step closer to being physical. By that I mean sex. Although he did indicate he was not into anything kinky, which on occasion I like, I'm not the cover-me-in-honey or dress-me-like-a-maid type of person. Instead, I like a variance in sexual positions. Jeremy was very uncomfortable when I raised the topic. Tantric sex was not his bag.

Having said that, we finally took the plunge and sex was had. Note how blandly I put that. It wasn't lust or love-making; it was just sex. To be honest, my vibrator would have given me the same level of satisfaction. Jeremy had a pulse and that was all.

It ended just like all the rest. The final straw was his constant attempts to try and speak French. This was charming to me for a while, but then it grated on me like listening to a loud American in a museum. But that is just me.

And personally, I don't like predictable. But I do like to be organized. I like knowing what I'm doing, and when I am doing it. But I also like surprises. It irritated me when Jeremy asked me out on a Sunday, and I informed him that I was busy. As a result, he spiralled into self-doubt and made such a scene. I mean, we all have our Sunday routine, right? Mine was laundry, paying bills, chilling in front of a good Netflix drama, or meeting with my girlfriends for brunch. I don't think there is anything wrong with that.

But one thing is clear to me. I am a serial Tinder dater, and I will just have to live with that. Or, should I, perhaps, give up?

SWIPE 12

Captain America

This story is different from the others in this book because it's not set in Singapore, but Los Angeles. So, where shall I start? I guess at the beginning. But first, some imagery to set the scene.

Captain America, as we all know, is a fictional character. He is the epitome of American values and identity. The USA is falling apart. Washington, D.C. has been decimated by some strange force. The US government is in turmoil. States have broken away from the union and have formed coalitions or alliances. This is the backstory behind *Ultimate Comics* 'Divided we Fall, United We Stand'. On the brink of destruction, America needed a symbol, a uniting factor. America needed a hero to rise to the challenge and lead the people to bring this great nation back to what it once was. Who was to heed the call of the American people? Well, none other than Captain America himself? Sounds like a familiar movie plot, right?

At the point when Donald Trump took his seat as president, America was, indeed, deep in crisis—its citizens were divided, mistrustful, nervous, and scared. Certain members of the

American population wanted Trump to lead them back to be a superpower.

> I ask America to look within themselves. My grandmother always said, ask not for challenges equal to our strengths, but for strength equal to our challenges . . . I look at America right now, broken, in pieces, and I remember—I once risked everything to answer a call. I realize now I can do more to serve my country. I know I can do more to live up to my potential. This crisis calls us all to do our best. To rebuild our fragile unity. To find strength equal to our challenges. I have decided to answer the call of the people. I accept. I, Steve Rogers—Captain America—do solemnly swear that I will faithfully execute the Office of the President of the United States. And will, to the best of my ability, preserve, protect, and defend the Constitution of the United States.

No, Donald Trump did not say those words, but Captain America did, and many wanted Trump to be their hero. Many of course did not, but that is a whole different story.

Now back to the start of our story. Monica shared her story with me over a long Skype call—several calls in fact, and far too many cups of coffee given the time zone difference. We were introduced via a mutual friend who had shared that I was writing another book. Monica, I was told, could not wait to share her story with me. It began when Monica matched with a man named Bill on Tinder, while she was strolling along Venice Beach. She recalled beaming a wide smile because Bill like the rugged all-American man in his profile picture.

How does one describe an all-American man, I asked out loud. My own image was of a beefy guy in his teens or twenties wearing shoulder pads and a football helmet. So, Monica tried to explain: an all-American man or woman has all the good qualities that many in the US consider typical of Americans; for example, being attractive, healthy, and hard-working. It wasn't the most exciting description I had heard, but hey, to Monica that was how Bill seemed—tanned, healthy, handsome, and hard-working.

The messaging commenced and they started to get to know each other. Likes, dislikes, passions, interests, and everything in between. Bill, it seemed was a true man's man—he loved sport, hunting, beer, and being American. Monica was not so American, in that she was from Canada.

I asked Monica how she would describe the difference between the two cultures, despite the similarity in accent. But even that would be challenged I am sure.

'Neither is true, of course, although Canadians, very generally speaking, tend to be more passive than Americans, who will often speak loudly and aggressively to make themselves heard. Canadian meeting culture is more like the culture in Britain, with people speaking in turn.'

But for Monica and Bill, that fine line between them when one gets accused of being the other was a big deal. To them, it's like calling an Australian a New Zealander. It was at that point Monica realized just how patriotic Bill was, as he went on to share how great he thought Donald Trump was. His view was something along the lines of Trump has taken the greatest office an American can hold, the Office of the President of the United States. It will be his duty now to not just protect the American people but lead them and guide them. He is the face of all that America stands for from his star-spangled underpants to his values and heroism. He was Bill's hero, elected to uphold the patriotic fervour that represents America for what it is. To be fair, Monica did ask for his view, and she most certainly got it!

Monica recalled their first date. She was seated at a café in West Hollywood reading a newspaper. A huge Dodge Ram truck pulled up in the cark par, and she could see Bill seated behind the wheel. His head sported a faded baseball cap with some logo or other and he flicked a wave. Monica waved back as Bill climbed down from the truck and seemed to vanish behind the door. Bill, it turned out, despite his large vehicle was short in stature. He walked over, hugged her, and took a seat.

The conversation was about the state of the nation as Bill yet again showed his passion for America. At one point, Monica expected him to produce a six-shooter and start firing it off into the air. Monica felt uneasy. It wasn't because Bill was rude, quite the opposite. It was more his racist views, and it seemed that anyone who was not white American was an alien to him.

Just as the third cup of coffee had arrived, Monica decided to test Bill's limits of self-control by talking about Canada and the advantages it had over good old USA. After that, she commented on what she considered to be the differences between Canada's Prime Minister Justin Trudeau and US President Donald Trump. But before she could barely utter a few words, Bill jumped in. 'That guy is a two-faced liar, that's what he is.' Monica paused mid-sip of her coffee.

'Have you ever met Mr Trudeau?' She asked.

'Nope. Don't care to neither.' Bill puffed up his chest.

Monica proceeded to enquire further knowing she had pushed a button and wanted to see if Bill would self-destruct. Bill continued with accusations and examples of how Trump was far superior to Trudeau and that America would become great again as a result. One could argue what does 'great' look like? Canada, in Bill's view, was a puppet nation and confused about whether to be French or British. And as a result, Canadians were of low intellect in his opinion. Monica after an hour of this debate had had enough. It was time to detonate Bill and leave.

'So, given your passion for the USA, why would you even consider dating me? Someone of low intellect.' She fired off the question. Bill took it right between his blue eyes and his jaw dropped.

Monica recalled Bill sitting frozen for a good long while. He seemed like a deer that had been shot, perhaps by one of his red-neck friends. Then, he simply got up from his seat, boarded his monster truck, and drove away. Captain America, it seemed had met his match in Monica, in more ways than one.

SWIPE 13

Romeo

Romeo, Romeo, where art thou Romeo? Deny thy father and refuse thy name; or if thou will not, be but sworn by my love . . . and so it goes on.

Okay, so Romeo Montague as most of us know was the main protagonist of William Shakespeare's well-known tragedy *Romeo and Juliet*. The son of Lord Montague and his wife, Lady Montague, secretly loves and marries Juliet, a member of the rival House of Capulet, through a priest named Friar Laurence. Forced into exile after slaying Juliet's cousin Tybalt in a duel, Romeo commits suicide upon hearing of Juliet's death. Now that may sound extreme, but the cost of love is sometimes very high indeed.

So, before I share Megan's story, indulge me for a moment. As a person who has done my fair share of dating, and picked up more than my fair share of dinner and drinks tabs over the years, I was thinking how much does it cost to find the real love of your life? A fortune, I hear you all scream!

For starters, the starting point is this: what does it cost to go out on a date, or be dating in general. Even if you're a woman who goes out on a lot of first dates and are expecting the man to pay, there is still a cost. It costs money to buy outfits, get your nails and hair done, and so on. If we don't get into the who-must-pick-up-the-tab discussion and look at the actual cost, it may surprise you.

According to a match.com survey, the annual cost of dating for a man is $1,855 and for a woman around $1,423. Not such a big gender gap, after all, it seems—at least, when it comes to dating. So, that covers the cost of dating, but how much does it cost to find the real love of your life?

Believe it or not, there is a company based in Canada that actually studies this every year, and you guessed it, the price tag is high. In a 2018 survey, it was estimated at a whopping $72,000.

Now let's get back to the entire process of what it actually costs to find the true love of your life. We know that dating apps are relatively cheap but what about the countless hours spent getting to know someone or going for first dates. This is a cost that maybe hard to calculate. For each of us, time has a different value but one thing is for sure, we can never get that time back. For a growing number of people, especially busy professionals or people burned out over the whole online dating world—being catfished, or meeting creeps, criminals, married people, and so on—the solution presents itself in the form of dating coaches or professional matchmakers. Dating coaches can be very helpful to hone your skills at weeding out the bad picks or learning to spot right away one who is *not* right for you. In that sense, a matchmaker can save time as they learn to understand you and your needs, and, in turn, can potentially find you a better match than you can on your own. Additionally, they can also save you precious time. But in big cities like New York City,

London, Singapore or Los Angeles, a good matchmaker can be very expensive. It is not uncommon to pay upwards of $25,000 in fees.

Also, don't forget the value of your time spent in sharing enough information with these professionals to help them do their job. As they say, you only get out what you put in. I have spoken to a number of women, even friends, who have wasted so much time, money, and energy on dating that the thought of an easier way, even if it comes with a hefty price tag, is welcome news. Dating coaches are also an option but they too are right up there in terms of their high fees. Besides, success rates vary and, I am told, only fifteen per cent of people who've used such services ended up with a marriage proposal.

So, when we ask how much does it cost to find the real love of your life, the answer depends on how much you value your time, or the actual monetary costs, or your sanity for that matter.

Now, to get back to the story in hand, which I know you are itching to read!

Early thirties, Australian, fair-haired, physically fit and standing at five feet four inches, Megan is a dynamo of a woman, and always seems to be in a rush. This is her story.

It was late, the supermarket was all but deserted as Megan rushed up to the checkout with a basket brimming with food items and toiletries. Her earbuds were booming the peppy song 'Dance Monkey', so she had a spring in her step. Megan paid for her groceries in cash, having not mastered the art of tap and go with her credit card yet, and set off to find a taxi. Some twenty or so minutes later, she was finally on her way home, despite the fact that the taxi smelt of old socks. To take her mind off the foul odour, she started to check her phone for any missed calls or messages. She was in luck, given an alert from a man calling himself Romeo, aged forty-two, who had matched with her on Tinder. The temptation to check the match immediately was too hard to resist. So, she logged into Tinder.

Now let's be honest here, Romeo is not a common name unless you are the son of a once famous Manchester United football star. In this instance, Romeo, by his own profile description was half French and half English, which probably meant he loved wine with his fish and chips. At least pre-Brexit!

As Megan digested his profile, which included four or five pictures of a well-groomed male in suits, smart casuals, and one of him in a tuxedo, shot in what seemed a yacht marina, her first reaction was 'too good to be true'. He was tanned and extremely handsome. In truth, Megan didn't recall swiping right on him at all. Yet here he was. His written profile introduction described him as single, fit, action-oriented, and he was a man of charm, ethics and not, in bold letters, a scam artist. He then confessed to having a job that was unusual and that he would share this upon meeting face to face. But first Megan needed to find out a little more and sent a message winging its way to Romeo. She confessed to me that she didn't hold out much hope that he would turn out to be genuine, but curiosity got the better of her. It took no more than thirty minutes for Romeo to reply, with a polite 'good evening'. From there the chat commenced and covered the basics. Yes, the obligatory, age, confirmation of declared single status, residential status, and so on. But the one question still unanswered was his occupation. Megan enquired and awaited the reply. It came the next day as Megan was sipping coffee with a friend. 'I'm self-employed.' Now, this reply triggered a great deal of chatter between Megan and her friend. It culminated in Megan's friend, Jane, telling her she would be mad to continue as clearly something was amiss.

Undeterred, Megan agreed in her next stream of messages to meet Romeo face to face. She wanted above all to have some fun.

Finally, the day of the date was here. And as Megan took her seat, Romeo, aka David, opened with a confession. He did this before even ordering a drink. 'I'm a professional companion by the way, and my real name is David.' He smiled through his overly white teeth.

Megan contemplated the announcement before issuing her reply. 'First, I'll have a large gin and tonic, thank you. Second, you're telling me you are basically a gigolo? Unless you house sit for old ladies and their cat's kind of companion.'

Romeo ordered them both drinks and then replied. 'I prefer escort or companion. Gigolo is so distasteful. But yes, I am.' David leaned forward. 'So, I guess with that you will be leaving?'

Megan also leaned in. 'Hell no, I want to know all about it, all the dirty little secrets. Not that I'm in the market for one, you understand.' Megan had decided she may as well enjoy this unique experience. That and David had informed her, he was not all he seemed, caveated that he was not after anything bad. So, she had to respect his honesty. David laughed, relaxed back, and started to explain his life.

'I guess I create space where my clients can feel free to talk about their biggest fears and insecurities, knowing that I only have one primary goal—that being their happiness. In terms of therapeutic value, I beat any psychologist hands down. What psychologist would hold you in their arms?' David laughed.

Megan found him fascinating and urged him to continue as the gin finished and the wine flowed. This for her, was now far more exciting than a date with someone 'unextraordinary'.

David had a story, and it was drawing her in. He went on to explain that his clients told him things they would never ever share with a friend or partner. Time spent with a companion he believed had real benefits. At this juncture, Megan reminded him that to her, he was still a gigolo, but he should carry on regardless. He recounted how his clients were all older women, with one thing in common, they were all in loveless relationships. The time they spent with him, made them feel heard, respected, and free. He also pointed out that not all of his clients wanted sex rather a companion to talk to over dinner or drinks. When Megan showed a slight show of disbelief, David did confess that some did, indeed, spend the night with him.

As the hours ticked by, Megan listened intently. But given it had reached 1.00 a.m., she had reached her limit.

Megan left the date with something she had not expected. Not only did she have insight into the world of a gigolo, but also realized how many women had given up on being in a normal relationship because of myriad reasons such as divorce from cheating husbands, loveless marriages, abuse or just a relationship that had gone stale. She truly appreciated more than ever that she was single, and for now, she decided to stay that way. As for David, she never heard from him again and that was okay by her.

SWIPE 14

Catch Me if You Can

Yen, our protagonist for this story, was Singaporean, thirty-years old, physically fit, and worked for a private bank. She was in general terms a good catch. I say in general terms as some men, as she informed me, found her intimidating. Yen had been single for two years on account of her focus on work. Long hours and meeting clients had taken over her social time. Attending social gatherings alone was not something she wanted to continue. On the insistence of her friends, she signed up for Tinder to find a man. Her apprehensive dive into the online dating world had begun. But the old fashioned way of meeting someone had not eluded her, and one evening the stars in her world had seemed to have aligned.

'Beautiful here, isn't it?' were the first words Yen had heard from Duncan's lips. She turned slowly to eye him up and down and felt a small smile crack on her face. Duncan was an American—evident from his accent—standing at six-or-so-feet tall, broad-shouldered, well-dressed, and in good physical shape. His eyes were a hazel brown, and a greyish mop of short cut hair topped him off. He was most certainly not unattractive to Yen, and his smile was warm.

'Yes. It is.' Yen responded.

They were both standing atop of the Marina Bay Sands hotel in Singapore, on the sky deck—taking in the city vista below framed with lights—and by coincidence both sipping the in-house sparkling—pretending to be champagne—white wine. The conversation that followed was easy and relaxed as they each shared their obligatory introductions. Yen is nothing if not fiercely independent. Duncan, it seemed was not in the least intimidated as he continued to chat with ease. He was no slouch either, given his partner-level role in a large consulting firm.

As the evening wore on and came to a close at around midnight, Duncan played his cards. He announced that he wanted to see Yen again, this time over dinner. He then offered to share his phone number, which Yen accepted. But what happened next, took Duncan somewhat by surprise. Now before you query, yes, this book is about the female perspective. I have not forgotten, so hold your horses and read on.

Yen recounted to me when sharing her story that she loved games, and so it began with Duncan. Told you. The female perspective is back! Yen agreed to see Duncan again, but only if he could find her on Tinder and Yen in return matched with him. Now call me opinionated, but had I been Duncan, I would have said something like 'Are you serious?' But then again, this is not about me—it is Yen's story. Duncan agreed. Seems he was a sport and up for this challenge.

The term, needle in a haystack comes to mind. But I was informed it took Duncan a week to find Yen on Tinder and get a match back. They agreed to meet.

A few days after the match, a second date was on the cards—this time, dinner followed by cocktails. It was the perfect evening. But Yen was not done with her games. She informed

Duncan that should he wish to see her for a third time, she had another challenge. I asked Yen if Duncan was still the playful puppy and took it all in good spirit. Apparently, he was. I deduce from this that he was either desperate or just good fun. The challenge was set. Duncan had to find a bar, which was hidden behind a camouflaged door on a street that was named after a city with a white star ferry. He had to arrive the following Thursday evening at 8.00 p.m. Yen recalled thinking that any fool could crack this challenge. Clearly, she had low expectations of Duncan.

Duncan I'm told did find the bar and found Yen on a barstool at one end of the countertop. She congratulated him and they enjoyed an evening of cocktails and light finger food. Yen recalled that Duncan was as charming as ever. They agreed to meet again.

Yen wanted to continue her game and suggested a venue for dinner, only this time she sent Duncan a photograph, showing just a section of the restaurant's frontage. Duncan, it seemed was happy to play along. As the evening approached, Yen took efforts to look lovely and set off, making sure she arrived ahead of time. Upon her arrival at a small restaurant in Singapore's club street, she took her seat at the reserved table, ordered a glass of wine, and awaited the arrival of Duncan. A few minutes after 8.00 p.m.—the time they had agreed to meet—a staff from the restaurant approached her with a note in hand. The young man handed her the note and left. Yen read the note. She recounted the context to me, which basically said:

Dear Yen,

You are a playful and imaginative lady. I'm sure you could be much fun. While your little games could be perceived as refreshing and fun, everything has its limits, and I've reached mine. Perhaps you should take the time to get to know someone, rather than use them as a pawn in your next challenge. As you can see by now, if you are reading this note, I found the restaurant—now sit back, enjoy your dinner, and reflect.

Duncan

Yen had been played at her own game. She did reflect, but continues to play such games on her dates, and wonders if this is why she is still single.

SWIPE 15

True Lies

According to Wikipedia, the Central Intelligence Agency (CIA) is a civilian foreign intelligence service of the federal government of the US, tasked with gathering, processing, and analysing national security information from around the world, primarily through the use of human intelligence. Most of you know this unless you have been living under a rock. Some of us may have wondered what it would be like to work for such an agency, or at the very least watched a movie where the CIA is prominent in the plot.

The complex life of a CIA officer has been shared in many an article and portrayed in numerous films, often revealing an existence that is both terrifying and amusing, but never boring.

Enter Sarah, a British-born national, thirty-nine years old, living in Singapore, who by chance matched on Tinder with a man. We will refer to him as John. Let us skip past the preliminary messaging routine followed by the consent to meet. Why? Because you have heard it before, and this is far too good a story to delay sharing it.

So, imagine for a moment, that on your first date with John, when asking about his occupation, he informs you he was a former CIA agent. This is what Sarah recalls.

John shared that he was a CIA Case Officer who served in the Directorate of Operations (DO) with multiple tours in Afghanistan and throughout the Middle East. He was in Afghanistan throughout President Obama's 2010 Afghan Surge, during which time he claimed to have worked on eliminating the deadliest of improvised explosive devices (IED) networks in the world as well as the removal of numerous al-Qaeda and Taliban High Value Targets from the battlefield.

You can imagine that Sarah was a little shocked by this admission. She was expecting something far more conventional, such as banker or advertising exec, or even owner of a shipping company. She then wondered if John was faking it, but he seemed far too knowledgeable. Either that or he had watched way too many spy movies.

Sarah recalled at this point the movie *True Lies*, the one with Arnold Schwarzenegger and Jamie Lee Curtis. A secret agent's life takes a shocking turn when he learns about his wife's extramarital affair. He must now not only save the world but also his own marriage. She wondered if that would be her in years to come. No, of course not. She returned her focus back to John, who, she added, was not wearing a black balaclava to hide his identity.

Soon, John went on to describe an operation he was on, named Orion, which resulted in the capture of several Taliban warlords. His final assignment, he said was with a top-secret task force operating in Syria.

Sarah interjected and asked a question that I think anyone of us would have asked. 'Should you not discuss this sort of thing?'

John responded saying it was fine, given he had left the CIA a few years back. He was now a regular citizen. Now, this was a red flag to Sarah, given she too had watched way too many films on the subject and learnt that one never quite left the services of the CIA, once in. Or, at least, that's what she thought because it seemed far more covert and thrilling.

John chatted on, using enough acronyms to make Sarah's head spin. He had hidden his identity for ten years from everyone except his brother. It probably helped that he was single at the time with no kids. It was at this point that Sarah realized something was amiss. This all meant he was an expert in telling lies! Maybe he was real, or maybe just a good liar. She listened on while enjoying a fine bottle of Australian red wine.

Sarah recalled asking him a question. 'How did you hide it from your family?'

John thought for a moment. 'Since you asked about family—I classify that as solely my mom, dad, and brother. And, yes, I kept it from my parents by telling them I was a sales guy for an insurance company—which I also told everyone else—and since that's boring, there weren't a whole lot of other follow up questions to be honest. My brother played along.'

'Have you told them now?' Sarah asked.

'I told my mom and dad last year. It was a gigantic weight off my chest that I had been carrying for the past ten years.'

'So, you were a spy. How sexy.' Sarah announced.

John laughed. 'Spies can come from all walks of life. There are no skills that you can learn per se prior to joining the agency that will make you a stronger candidate. Yes, the military would help to a degree but in order to be a case officer, which is what

I was, you really can't prepare for that ahead of time. Which is a good thing. That way everyone is starting on a level playing field. Which, for me especially, was an advantage given that I was just an average guy from Texas.'

As the evening closed, Sarah could not decide if John was real or not. He certainly seemed it. So, having given him the benefit of the doubt, on the ride home, she decided to see him again. A second date was arranged a week or so later.

The day of the date arrived, a sunny Sunday. Sarah was dressed in shorts and a t-shirt. A casual café was the venue. Great coffee was on offer and John looked as relaxed as Sarah, in that he too was in shorts and a t-shirt. They sat on a comfortable sofa in one corner, so as not to be too surrounded by the other customers. Sarah had stored up some questions. She recalled what they were and shared them with me.

'Did you use a fake name?' She asked.

'Yes, I did. In fact, most of my friends still call me by my fake name even though they know my true name. Wild huh?' John mused.

Sarah wondered if his Tinder profile name was the fake name. She, of course, asked and John stated that John was his real name. Sarah wondered why he would have used a fake name in the CIA and his real one on Tinder. But she decided not to go there and continued with her next question.

'Was it all worth it? To live such a life.'

John didn't hesitate. 'I ask myself the same question every day. Was any of it worth it? Will the Taliban retake Afghanistan? They very well might. Will ISIS continue to grow? I think they are starting to decline but will someone else readily take their place depending on their motive? Yes, it was worth it.' John apparently, was more serious in this response.

Sarah at this point wanted to change the subject. She asked John why he had never asked much about her. It occurred to Sarah that the entire thread of their conversation had all been about him and his past.

John now struggled to respond. He seemed very uncomfortable as if he found small talk challenging.

Sarah shared her life, hobbies, and what she wanted in a relationship. None of which seemed to excite John. In fact, Sarah recalls thinking that he looked rather bored.

Something still wasn't feeling right. Was this some elaborate story to impress her? Or was it that John simply got a kick out of telling a web of stories. Sarah level checked herself by recalling that when confronted with a lie, the best approach is to fact-check and get some solid evidence before calling someone out. What if he was real? She would feel so bad. Worse, he could kill her! Okay, perhaps that was taking it a tad too far. But she still had no idea how he would react. Sarah decided to call the date to an end and promised to contact him soon. On the way home, she hit Google and tried to research the CIA and how to detect if someone is telling you a lie.

This is what she managed to learn in the twenty-minute journey back home. When we suspect, we've been lied to, we might start to look for telling signs such as avoiding eye contact, changes in routine and behaviour, and stories and excuses that don't add up.

Sarah needed to find a motive. What would John have to gain by lying to her? He certainly had not tried to get her into bed. So, it appeared that his motive was not sex. Did John have a reason to lie? Was what he was telling her plausible? She did not think so. It wasn't a normal occurrence to date a CIA agent.

Sarah had no idea what to do next, other than she liked him. He seemed nice and had not shown any bad motive. But Sarah knew one thing, she simply had to ask him for solid proof. If not, any chance of a relationship based on trust would be impossible. Her reasoning was solid. What John had shared was deep and not the normal life any man would lead, unless you are of course a bona fide CIA agent. She believed it was worth the energy to find out the truth. To her, the truth, or lack thereof, could be a deal-breaker. It would eradicate any hope for a future relationship based on trust.

A few days later Sarah called John and posed the question, 'Are you real?' explaining her need to understand, and why she felt it a reasonable enough question to ask. John, Sarah recalled, was adamant in that everything he had shared was true. He was calm, not offended, and seemed to understand. Sarah went to bed happy that evening in the knowledge that she believed him. All was well.

The story ends with a twist. Sarah never heard from John again. His number was changed. His Tinder profile was deleted, and he simply vanished. Sarah wonders to this day, was he real or not? Every Tinder date since then, she says, has been somewhat boring.

SWIPE 16

Ironman

If you were asked to think about the word 'Ironman', you would probably either think of an ironman athlete, who fearlessly takes part in a series of long-distance triathlons and looks something like a greyhound in physique, dressed in skin-hugging lycra—or, you would think of a man in a red tin suit from Hollywood. Yes, the actor Robert Downey Jr is an image many would think of.

For Zoe, it was the former. Tim, a native New Zealander looked every inch the ironman athlete in his profile. Dressed in black lycra, super skinny physique, straddling a carbon fibre bicycle while cycling up a hill that looked almost vertical. He was thirty-six years of age and totally bald. Zoe adds here that she was not an iron-woman; in fact, quite the opposite. The hardest thing she did for social exercise was lifting her latte coffee and when there was an eclipse of the sun, went for a jog that lasted no more than fifty metres. Not that Zoe was overweight, far from it.

Singaporean, attractive and single, Zoe had much to offer. Her career as a banker afforded her with a good lifestyle and socially, she was very active. She simply liked fit men and Tim fitted the bill perfectly. But Zoe was under no illusions when she had matched with Tim on Tinder. She knew it may be tough and compromises would have to be made. If not, it would be a match from hell.

Before Zoe and Tim actually met and started dating, the only ironman she had known, some three years' prior, was a former work colleague. He had quit his job six months before a race and devoted all of his time to training. While she thought that was extreme, the thought of dating someone skilfully balancing a full-time job, which Tim had as a software developer, training, and entering a new relationship was still a little intimidating. She wondered why he was on Tinder if he had so little time to devote to getting to know someone. Undeterred, she pressed on and agreed to meet him. After all, what harm would meeting him do? Besides, if all else failed, there was always Robert Downey Jr!

The first date went really well, and it was followed by a second. Their chemistry was on fire, and they seemed at ease with each other. Tim then openly shared that he would have his next race in six-months' time, so his training would start soon and his diet would mean little to no alcohol. Zoe seemed relaxed about it and all seemed well. Zoe wanted to understand more, which Tim happily shared. He had always been active and had run a few half marathons, but he also preferred activities like yoga, hiking, and a leisurely swim. He made a point of clarifying that he was not the type of maniac that did weekly 100-km bike rides and daily 2-km swims. Yet, it wouldn't to be farfetched to state that Zoe wasn't exactly interested in the same things as Tim.

Tim accepted this, but encouraged her to, perhaps, at least, try yoga. The very next week, Zoe attended a beginner's class and loved it. Tim, it seemed was having a positive influence.

Over the next month or so, Zoe began to realize what it actually meant to date this type of man. She recalls that Saturday nights were spent on the couch watching Netflix, and they were often in bed by 10.00 p.m. To an ironman, Saturdays were meant for hard, long workouts, icing the body and eating lots of carbohydrates. After eight hours straight of intense exercise, going out to dinner, dancing wasn't really an option. Zoe loved to dance and when she needed a night out, she called upon her select group of girlfriends. That said, she found herself starting to enjoy cosy nights on the couch with Tim, just as she enjoyed hanging out with her friends. Was she changing her outlook on life she wondered? She also discovered she was becoming a morning person given Tim's weekends started at 5.00 a.m., just like the weekdays when he was in full training mode. Now you may wonder why that would impact Zoe. Well, she had started to spend more time at his home. It was getting serious.

It wasn't long before Zoe had counted how long she had been seeing Tim since their match on Tinder. It had been six months. This for Zoe was a personal best given she had typically moved on from boyfriends after just six weeks. She had become hooked on Tim and had by now become a regular at the yoga studio and even started to ride a bicycle. Inevitably, some part of his body was always hurt from exhaustion, a pulled muscle, or minor injuries. The difficult part was remembering just which part it was every day. On Mondays, it might have been, 'Watch out for my left shoulder and walk only on my right side so I can put my arm around you.'

A few days later, the shoulder might be better, but instead, it would be, 'Be careful not to touch my knee with the big bruise.' Zoe also went through a couple of months of a blister problem, so that was, 'Let's not go anywhere that requires walking more than fifteen steps or wearing a strappy sandal.' She found it hard keeping track of injuries of each day but was easily reminded with the frequent 'Ouch'.

This all meant of course that their love life was non-existent during training, and this was something that Zoe had not learned to come to terms with so readily. Just two days before his race—when Tim yet again refused to make love due to not wanting to injure himself, Zoe snapped saying it was not as if she was expecting acrobatics in bed! Zoe walked out and left Tim to it.

Weeks passed and all had gone silent between them. Zoe had even dropped yoga. That was until Tim turned up unannounced on her doorstep one evening, flowers in hand and sporting his triathlon medal. Zoe recalled the night was spent making love and all seemed wonderful again. Tim apologized and promised not to be so intense in the future and consider her needs as well . . . at least until the next training season began!

Zoe and Tim went on to get married, and this demonstrates that Tinder does have its successes. Though Zoe never went back to yoga or the bicycle, she is happy and Tim is still very much her ironman.

BONUS SWIPE 1

Awaken the Queen

This story is different from the other stories in this book—and, not due to the fact that the couple met as a result of a 'Super Like' on Tinder. No, it's because I, as the writer of this story, met someone that really understood who she was as a person. This woman was Tegan, a forty-one-year-old Australian woman. By her own self-description and admission, she was built like a bus and wore dresses. She even joked that her dresses could be rented out as event marquees under which people would sip tea. And she enjoyed nothing more than a good steak. Harsh I told her, having observed within moments of meeting her that she had something far greater than physical prowess. Her energy and zest for life were apparent—so apparent in fact, that you cracked a smile just by being in her presence. Tegan was despite her own harsh description, a very beautiful woman. She had this glow about her. Tegan opened her discussion with me like this:

> 'I used to go on dates praying the guy would like me and not judge me. I now go on dates hoping the queen inside of me will like him.' She beamed a monumental smile.

I settled back with my flat-white coffee, opened up my ears and asked Tegan to just let rip and talk. Something she had no problem in doing. In fact, I had to ask her to draw a breath once in a while as word after word escaped her lips in rapid fire and became absorbed into my memory. This was again a different experience for me. During other interviews, I had to really provoke responses by asking multiple questions, trying to structure the conversation and extract the story. Yes, pulling teeth springs to mind. But with Tegan, her download flowed like the Tigris in full winter flood.

'A few Sundays ago, I went on a date. I had super liked this cute guy, and we matched—a writer like you—through a dating app. Yes, I sometimes end up on them.' Tegan mused and then continued.

'When he invited me out, I told myself why not, the weather was great, I had washed my hair. I also told myself it was time to practice my newly discovered inner queen self-love.'

I listened intently as she spoke, taking copious notes, realizing of course that she was on a mission. Not a mission to find a man or have a sordid encounter, but to discover her inner self. It was so refreshing to listen to her. Here was a woman, not just talking about her dating experience but sharing what she truly wanted to discover about herself. She could recall every detail of her date. No stone was left unturned.

Tegan explained that she felt a deep connection with the man that Sunday and without being cliché, nor being fake about it, she felt after having seen him a few times since, that he adored her.

'He loved every inch of me, wholesomely, even the hair in my armpits, my smell, my skin. Every inch.'

I add here that I almost spat out my coffee when Tegan mentioned her armpits. Way too much

information, and I just had to take a peek at that point—to verify if the hanging gardens of Babylon were, indeed, resident under her arms. Thankfully, they were not.

Either that, or Tegan had taken a garden strimmer and dealt with the issue before meeting with me.

Anyway, I regained my composure and asked her to continue. After a half-hour or so, I deduced that every interaction she had with this man was conscious. Meaning she was in control of her thoughts at every moment. Tegan agreed and admitted that she had never been so intimate with someone while being so present and mindful, which meant, I deduced, being sober at the time. And that she had never met a man who venerated her as much as he did. He filled her it seemed with so much appreciation. I almost wanted to meet him myself, given he was a writer, but half expected to come face to face with a superhero in a tight-fitting outfit carrying a dustbin lid! His superpowers had certainly won Tegan over. It was then when I had a twinge of concern. I hoped this story would not end up with her being scammed or hurt in some way. In any case, I allowed her to continue—in anticipation of the twist I assuredly expected in this so-called fairy tale. Genuine or not, what this man had done was build her self-esteem. He had awakened her inner queen—the very thing Tegan wanted. So much so that Tegan recalled one day looking at herself in the mirror and screaming out loud: 'I feel so sexy!'

I, of course, wanted to know more and asked Tegan to explain.

'He showed me what it was to honour a woman, to see in her the Goddess she truly is.'

If I'm honest, I did feel a bit nauseous with that reply, but then I wondered if this man was just good with words . . . given he was a writer. Or, did he have real substance? Just as I was about to ask, Tegan beat me to the punch and explained.

Knowing this man wrote for a living, advertising apparently, Tegan confirmed that she too had her initial doubts about his sincerity. But more importantly, she had made a promise to herself even before the first date, in that she was going to be herself, a 100 per cent, with this dude. He'd better have either a lot of humour, or a lot of masculine energy in him or be well-read about the world and self-development. Otherwise, Tegan shared, he would probably be a self-absorbed twat who drove a Porsche.

I stopped Tegan here and asked her to go back to the first date. I wanted to capture the details—the setting, the mood, the conversation. Tegan happily obliged, and this is what I deduced.

They had met at a café. Tegan and Pete— I now knew his name, he was not now just a man or the writer, he was Pete the writer. Tegan was sipping wine, while Pete ordered a beer.

Pete had openly started talking about himself and his work as a copywriter in advertising. Tegan and Pete asked each other a number of questions indulging in, what I like to call, the habitual nuptial dance of dates. Tegan talked about her battles with self-confidence, self-love, and acceptance. Her tone and voice she stated were grounded and not emotional. Her words came from the heart. She was not saying things to gain sympathy but genuinely sharing her story. Tegan then stopped mid-sentence, and I enquired what was wrong. Tegan drew a breath and informed me that Pete had taken her hand, and declared that he had always been looking for someone that made him feel euphoric. This was followed by Pete stating that he believed Tegan had an inner queen waiting to be set free! Her reaction was naturally priceless. Jaw dropped, smile erupted, warm fuzzy feeling. She could not recall exactly what she had replied, but something along the lines of 'wow, you can see that so soon?'

Later that evening Tegan had reflected. She had finally met someone who could see beyond her physical looks. He could see her confidence. Many people Tegan had met in the past judged her as being over-confident. And really, she said, it's a fine line. Tegan then shared her point—the point of her journey of self-change and discovery.

'By honouring the queen in you does not make you a self-absorbed bitch. The inner queen in you does not come from ego', she continued.

I was learning something new by listening to her. Activating the divine feminine, that powerful stream of energy within, is transformational. Yet, it is misinterpreted by many. Tegan blamed pop culture and its veneration of extremes and ego-exciting personas for the narrow-mindedness of people. When a woman is empowered—she is 'bossy', she is a 'badass'. Tegan had learned one thing early in life that most of the time, people judge on nuances, instead of extremes.

'We don't need to be Beyoncé to be an empowered woman,' she said.

I also learned from Tegan that to be sitting in the seat of the 'queen', as she liked to call this process, is actually pretty far from the exaggerated image we get of successful women in the media. The way Tegan explained it made complete sense. It's not about turning men into our servants. It's not about finding a sugar daddy. It's not about being bossy like the editor in *Devil Wears Prada*, and it's certainly not about actually dressing like a queen (although, you obviously can, if you fancy!). Extremes, extremes, extremes! Ego, ego, ego!

We're not supermen and superwomen. We're humans, yes with a spirit inside, but still, humans. It's about loving someone with all their attributes *and* yet, knowing our values and what we deserve.

It's about being strong *and* vulnerable. A goddess *and* a human being. It's about embracing all the facets of femininity—the strength and the softness (Kali and Laxmi), the brain and the heart, the darkness and the light. And, as cliché as this may sound, it all starts with self-love. The queen as I learned, comes from your deeper self, beyond the shallowness of the ego. Tegan then said something very real. She simply said that she deserved the best.

'I only understood there was a queen in me when I started loving myself. Honestly, six months ago, when I looked in the mirror and devoured my body with my eyes in admiration . . .' Tegan gave me another one of her missile smiles.

'This self-love goes way beyond the affirmations I used to stick on my bathroom mirror, mere motivational words masking my discomfort with myself. There is duality in being a spiritual being and living a human experience. And we must embrace it in order to thrive. I'm talking about feeling it . . . feeling it . . . inside. I'm talking about falling in love with yourself. It's a process that took me months and may take me years to master. And it's not flawless nor complete. But damn, do I notice the difference compared to who I was two years ago.' Tegan drew a breath. Which I thanked her for, as I was trying to keep up with my notes and understand what she was saying. Tegan had given me writing gold.

It was the perfect time for me to then explore what she was like before she started out on this journey of self-discovery.

'I let people abuse my time, my space, my body. I thought that being feminine meant to wear make-up and dress nicely. I dressed/acted/wore my hair according to external approval. My sexuality was okay as long as it was contained. I couldn't be too strong, especially not with men.'

'Now, I am a queen, I love my regal body—and I really do, with the fat, with the weird hair, with the smells and sounds, the juiciness, everything. I respect my time, space, and body because they are sacred. I love people, but I don't hesitate to cut them off if they're toxic towards me. I decide now what to do with my body, my hair, the way I dress, No one can ever tell me what to do with my vagina and my sexuality. I take care of me now. I am my own source of divine energy. I know I am not *just a woman*. I am part of a sisterhood composed of the women living now and the ones who lived before me, and I carry this heritage with me.'

At this juncture, I asked Tegan how Pete dealt with this transformation. Did he understand it? Did he support her? I was soon cut off at the knees. Pete not only understood and supported her, he had helped her by not questioning her motive. Pete had from the get-go accepted her for who she was before they had met in person and liked her physical form—even her armpits. He had boosted her ego and made her feel special. It seemed that Pete was everything she described and more. How wonderful I thought that she had met someone online, and for once he was not a fake or a cheat or a scammer. This was indeed a perfect match. Tegan and I had an hour or so left before I vanished into the black hole we writers descend into to write her story. So, I asked her what else she would like to impart. And, of course, she did have more for me.

'I have a myriad of facets: the wolf woman, the shaman, the queen, the mother, the sister, the daughter, the lover, the wife, the mistress, the builder, and the destroyer. *I look empowered from the outside, and I feel the same inside.* A man can have the privilege of bathing in my presence if his presence is aligned with mine. What I mean here is that I can allow a man in my energetic and physical field only if his mindset, vibe, and energy are at the same level as mine. What I don't mean is: "He'd better offer me things and pay for dinner if he wants to get this juicy body!" What I mean is that I am conscious of my worth as a divine creature. I practice physical connection in a conscious way—aware that it is an energy exchange. I seek a man that has this same mindset and who will know how to adore the queen I am, just as I will know how to adore the king he is.'

At this point, I requested a break. I wanted to make sure I understood her. I wandered off while she tended to her messages. I read my notes and contemplated everything. When I rejoined her a half-hour later, I asked her to just listen.

This is how I summed it up.

'Tegan', I said, 'two observations that make you your own queen, and I'm saying it from the heart.'

The first 'you' it's another layer of lies we tell ourselves to mask discomfort or negative self-judgments. It's like eating chocolate or watching Netflix when we don't feel well—it's a quick fix. It's a projection we make on others, and the others are doing so too. And at the end of the day, we're just a bunch of egos having conversations, and we spend our lives missing out on the real stuff—deep meaningful connections with fellow humans.

The second 'you' will fill your entire being with so much love and peace that it will radiate from within. People will see there is something different about you, and your light will attract them. So, you can share your love and light with them, spreading self-love and mindful connections around you, and connecting deeply with people, including romantic connections.

After this summary, I observed Tegan's face drop. Had I offended her? I held the pause. She sat back. Then she sat forward. She then stood up, turned in a circle, then sat back down. She then placed a hand on my knee and said:

'My God, you really get me! Yes. Yes! That's it!'

The moral of this story is obvious. In sharing it with me, Tegan was trying to convince people (but really, herself) that we are all heroes and all have inner kings and queens. We are all worthy, and that we have the right to be confident and express our self-confidence, no matter how we are physically formed. That knowing your self-worth and expressing it shamelessly does not equal being a self-absorbed prick.

Tegan was an inspiration and her story is one of my favourites. The best thing of all, she married Pete, and they are both are doing really well. Tegan still eats steak. In closing, I hope I have done her story justice.

BONUS SWIPE 2

Excuse Me

Allow me to set the scene for this next story. It will again be told by the lady as if she is speaking to you directly. I know that when I heard it, I had to bite my tongue and not laugh. Bad on me.

This story is about Katya, a very extroverted woman in her thirties.

Also, she was bisexual. Yes, this was how she first introduced herself. Which was cool. In fact, it would add an interesting lens to her experiences—and to mine narrations in this book.

And, so she began.

In 1825, a French noblewoman disturbed her high-society community when she began to uncontrollably yell obscenities during social engagements. A few years later, a French neurologist, Dr Georges Gilles de la Tourette, observed similar behaviour in a handful of young men. They'd shriek, grunt, or swear with abandon at anyone around them, sometimes when even alone. The good doctor labelled the syndrome *maladie des tics*, later renamed after himself as Gilles de la Tourette illness. It's what we now call today Tourette Syndrome, a condition characterized by the repetitive, involuntary movements and vocalizations known as 'tics'. Initially, doctors believed it was a psychological condition, but when patients responded to medication it became clear that a disease of the central nervous system.

Most early Tourette Syndrome sufferers were men not women. When observed in women, it was considered hysteria—the nineteenth-century feminine mental illness *du jour*. To this day, men are affected three to four times more often by Tourette's than their female counterparts. About 200,000 Americans have severe Tourette's, but one in a hundred are affected by milder forms of this condition. Symptoms usually start in the early teens and improve with age, and despite stereotypes of out-of-control maniacs who can't stop slapping their faces or yelling obscenities, people with Tourette syndrome reality experience a variety of tics ranging from throat-clearing, grunting, jumping, stroking objects, hissing, hooting, and blinking. Typically, these tics come and go and often deeply situational. In fact, the Tourette's poster child—the swearing tic known as coprolalia—only presents itself in about 10 per cent of those with the syndrome.

I matched on Tinder with one of the 10 per cent. His name was Ryan, a handsome forty-year-old half-French half Englishman.

On our first date he impressed me, he openly confessed that he had Tourette Syndrome for as long as he could remember. Some of the first tics he developed were that he felt tingling in his toes and fingers, and sometimes he would shake his head from side to side. He couldn't explain why. He did, of course, realize that this wasn't normal behaviour for people around him. However, he was lucky in that his parents were wonderful about it and got him the best possible care.

When Ryan was seven, he was also diagnosed with OCD, another condition that comes with many stereotypes. I remembered from a voluntary training I had done in the UK that it's actually common for people with Tourette's to have other disorders such as OCD or ADHD. The compulsion is similar to a Tourette tic, which feels like an insane itch that you just have to eventually scratch. I add at this point that I too started to feel itchy. It was that moment when someone tells you about an illness and you also feel the symptoms too. But I pulled myself together and listened, for no other reason than it was refreshingly honest and interesting. Here was man being so open it was kind of scary, but I respected him for it nonetheless. In fact, it was far better than the other dates I had been on.

He then let loose with an expletive and drew the attention of the people around us. I took his hand, squeezed it, and asked him to carry on. I had suddenly become Mother Teresa, the little frail nun that saved people in need.

He had counted at least fifty of his tics. He then joked that, with so many, it was amazing he got anything done. But, luckily, not all of his tics are present at the same time. He said that they would come and go as they please, visiting him every now and then. Plus, he had become really skilled at incorporating his Tourette tics into his daily life in a way that was socially acceptable.

Ryan further went on to explain that he had taught himself all kinds of ways to act on the urges to a point that they were not too disruptive to those around him. Not that he had managed to do this a few moments ago, but I listened on. He gave an example. For instance, if he had the urge to make a very large motion with his arms, or with his head, or make a very loud noise, he would address it by doing something a little bit lower on the scale. He would just clear his throat or sniff instead of making a high-pitched dolphin noise that some people might be a little bit surprised to hear, at best. Another way he explained was to camouflage his tics by pretending to brush his hair out of his face, and while doing so, he would squint his eyes really hard or whatever the urge was. Later, when he had some privacy, he would allow himself to go crazy with his louder tics and generally just 'tic out' completely! I must confess I did move my chair back an inch or two.

He then got to the point. He admitted that, of course, his Tourette's could be a huge nuisance, and it's not to say that it hadn't caused him embarrassment or anxiety, but since this was the only brain he known and understood, he did not want to be ashamed of it. That is the reason he didn't want to hide the fact that he had Tourette's when he met me. Ryan said that he had realized over the years that everybody must deal with their own 'thing'—whether it's a neurological disorder (as in his case) or simply that they've always been self-conscious about the shape of their nose. I admit at this point I touched my own nose and wondered if it was okay—I may poke it into people's business, but it was still a nice nose!

Ryan then made a comment that was really cool. He explained that when he was on a first date or meeting somebody at a party and he was hitting it off, he would go ahead and put it out there. He needed to assess how a woman reacted because to him it was like a built-in barometer to gauge someone's character. He called it his 'dating gauge' for sussing out potential partners. While he had never had, anyone run away screaming, he could tell if it made the person feel uncomfortable. And I get that. It's human nature to hide who we really are in some ways, especially those parts of us that make us feel insecure because as soon as you reveal your insecurities, you feel vulnerable. And being vulnerable is really scary. I considered this. I was not scared—more impressed really. Besides, I told him I couldn't run away in any case given the height of the heels I was wearing. He at least laughed.

He thought that the sooner you got to the vulnerable stuff, the faster you could figure out whether or not it was a good match. So, the Tourette discussion was a good way to weed out the ladies who weren't going to be a good fit. Also, in most cases, he found that his talking about Tourette's empowered the woman to also open up about things that she wouldn't have otherwise. Often, the other person also has a 'weird' thing, and the whole conversation turned into a lovely bonding moment. Now that made me think.

The date ended with me giving him a peck on the cheek and going home alone. I had much to think about. Here was a guy that was honest, open, and intelligent. He was intelligent because he knew himself. I wanted to see him again, at least as a friend, but wasn't sure at all about dating. A few days went by and I invited him out, just the two of us. I was not yet prepared for a social occasion, so lunch it was, one Saturday afternoon.

As we chatted about the weather, I decided it was my time to open up. Time for him to listen. I took him through the series of serial dates I had and why they had failed. He asked why I went on dates so soon after the preceding one had failed. I told him it had become habitual. I knew I needed to beak the habit, but how? Delete Tinder? No that would be like casting away my iPhone! I simply couldn't do that. Ryan found this amusing. I then noticed something—he hadn't set off a tic. I didn't want to ask him why, but I did observe that he was relaxed and maybe, just maybe, I was good for him. But I spoke too soon—an arm went skywards, and an expletive came out followed by a noise I can only describe as sounding like a harpooned dolphin. Well, that's what I thought it to be at the moment though I had obviously never harpooned a dolphin! Anyway, I hadn't recalled being called that name *a female dog* in a while, so I was a bit shocked. He apologized and we continued. He asked me to explain what I thought a serial dater was.

I explained to him that the serial dater is someone who refuses to play by the rules that we've all silently laid down as good conduct when dating. I loved the thrill of the chase and the first couple of dates; I relished that 'new date' feeling. I did emphasize that in the bizarre world of romance that exists today—the 'hook-up culture', if you will—there are three types of people: the lovers, the loners and, of course like me, the serial daters. But I was not in any way into hook-ups. He wanted to know more about how I perceived myself. So, I attempted to explain. At least my view on the three types I had identified.

The 'lovers' are exactly what one would think they are: hopeless romantics who long for an everlasting relationship with their soulmate and who will stay involved with 'the one' for months and months, or even years, without a second thought. They *need* consistent companions and manipulate their lives into ensuring that almost every aspect of their well-being revolves around the other person.

The 'loners' are the people who don't believe in relationships because they're *way* too good to be involved with someone else while they're working towards a career and trying to get their lives together. They're the ones who might go on a date or two every few weeks but believe the right person will walk into their lives when they aren't looking—if only that were true . . .

They're comfortable in their own skin and the person they've become and don't feel the need to search for someone to date.

And, then, of course, there are those like me—the serial daters. In world of romance, they are possibly the most dangerous of the three dating types. They're the tricky ones who will sweep you off your feet with witty charm and romantic execution and then leave you bewildered when you run into them the next day at a bar with their arms wrapped around another person. At this point, I had a eureka moment and realized I was talking about myself!

Serial daters are *never* left without a number to call or a person to text and pounce from one potential partner to the next, almost instantaneously. I, of course, had Tinder as my little black book. I would leave a man shocked and sometimes hurt when they realized what an insignificant aspect of my life they were. They were simply the pick of the day, maybe even the flavour of the week. At this point, I felt a pang of guilt. Ryan had opened me up like a tin of cat food, and I was spilling my guts. Not even a priest in confession had got me to talk so openly. And to cap it all off, not a tic in sight from Ryan. He was as cool as a cucumber. He then offered an observation. He said that if I was able to handle the one-and-done lifestyle of a serial dater, by all means, I should date away.

We ordered more drinks. It was going to be a long afternoon. He wanted to know what I liked best about being a self-proclaimed serial dater. I told him it was the honeymoon phase that I was addicted to. Undoubtedly, it is the best stage of a relationship. It is a time of vulnerable excitement and uncontrollable nerves, of course, and good sex! That sweet giddiness around each other, butterflies in the stomach, and that feeling of hard and fast into love. This is when memories are made. The fancy dinners on

Friday nights, and he'll even hold the door for you! Then you'll go out for drinks at an adorable cocktail bar and take fun trips to destinations you've both always dreamt to visit. You'll post Instas of the two of you—hand-in-hand—every chance you get. But, as expected, the honeymoon phase can be addictive and serial daters like me are most definitely the addicts. In fact, I had become *so* addicted to the honeymoon phase that I wanted to experience it over and over again with someone new almost every week. Sometimes multiple times in the same week. I had become completely enthralled with the excitement of a new kiss or a personality constantly craved a change of company. I looked at Ryan at this point. He was different for sure. I then confessed to 'Father' Ryan that my attention spans were short and my uncanny ability to walk out in and out of someone's life without a second thought was shocking. Ryan then let off a tic in the form of an arm wave. It did at least get us the attention of the waiter and another round of drinks. I continued.

I need someone better; I need something new and if the guy I am seeing is not giving me the thrill I want and crave, I don›t get too attached. I was then probably just another Tinder profile they deleted, and they would be the same to me. In summary I hated being single, but also hated the thought of being in a relationship. I hated the thought of being alone and not having someone eagerly waiting by the phone to answer every text I sent. In effect, I had via Tinder an assembly line of lovers waiting patiently for their profiles to be matched. It's almost like the monkey bar effect—the thing you did as a kid in a playground and ended up with bleeding knees and elbows. Serial daters swing from bar to bar, pleasing as they go and leaving at their own will. Being single means falling off of the monkey bars and landing face-first on the ground, bewildered, dazed, and confused. I cannot be single because I don't know how to be. I hate being bored.

Time was getting on, and far too many drinks had been consumed. We parted ways with a hug and a kiss and agreed to meet again.

However, I was not done. I kept going over in my head what I had discussed with Ryan. Tinder stayed switched off in the taxi ride home, and I thought long and hard about who I had become. I was basically insecure as I constantly needed to date to maintain my confidence. I knew that this type of relationship could be very toxic. I was also acutely aware of the impact I may be having on those I dated, and it may have diminished their confidence. By falling victim to the ongoing need for admiration, I had begun to need that same amount of attention in order to be happy. The more I thought about it, I realized I was just like an alcoholic. Was there a clinic for serial daters, like alcoholics anonymous, I wondered? If there was, I should go, or maybe start one myself.

I reached home, had a gin and tonic, showered and tried to sum up everything up in my head. Stretched out on the sofa, I started to think. I had to learn to understand my self-worth and understand that I didn't need one person, or many, constantly around me.

In all this, my biggest downfall was my ongoing fear of commitment. I was jaded and didn't believe in everlasting love. So, I was filling my time with temporary men, or women if I was feeling really adventurous, to fill the void of a long-term relationship. I should explain the woman aspect too. Yes, I confess, I dated a woman, and it was amazing. I'd even go as far as to say that every woman should experience it. It was a real fifty shades experience and one I shall never forget.

As for Ryan, we met a few more times. He is a darling of a man who battles with his illness each and every day. We became good friends not lovers and I learned to laugh with him and ignore the onlookers each time his tic went off. He taught me something very special in that I looked deep into my own soul and realized who I was. Perhaps only a man that had done that himself could have triggered me to do the same. I am the better person for knowing him. I would never have imagined that a man I had met through Tinder could have had such an impact.

So, there you have it. Steer clear of me—the serial dater—if you're searching for something serious because I'm out on the prowl and ready to pounce.

Yet, if you're feeling brave and seeking a thrill, give one a chance. He or she will leave you on the edge of your seat, wondering what the next date will bring—if there is a next date. I may just match with you on Tinder.

And, if you're feeling wary, just keep my story in mind and stay aware of the one-and-done lifestyle those like me lead.

BONUS SWIPE 3

We Are Who We Are

This next story is important in so many ways. Not least because it is about courage. It's also about the sad world we live in—something most of us don't care to admit. Often at times, we choose to look the other way when faced with something for which we have no experience.

I walked away after this interview with a newfound level of respect for people in the same situation as Emily, the one whose story this is. When she wrote to me and asked if she could share her story, I, of course, said yes. But pause for a moment. Why did I say yes?

I said yes, because Emily shared she had used Tinder and been on a few dates. Most of her dates ended quickly, so quickly in fact that I wondered why. I wanted to know why most of the men she agreed to meet would leave within five minutes of her meeting them. Emily openly admitted this fact. What she did not share with me was why. I ask you to read this story with open eyes and an open heart. Then ask yourself what you would have done. It does not matter if you are male or female or anything in between. Just ask yourself and be honest.

Let me begin.

Emily, a thirty-three-year-old Singaporean, had the kind of face that made you instantly crack a smile. I knew this because she had sent me a photo. It was a close-up of her head and shoulders, taken at a beach somewhere. She worked as a freelance graphic designer and in her spare time wrote song lyrics. So, what could possibly be wrong with such a woman in the eyes of most men. Probably nothing at all. Most men have a type they like—dark skinned, long or short hair, big or small eyes, the list goes on.

I entered the café on time on the day I was to meet Emily. I took my seat opposite her and knew instantly why some men would have left their date with her. I add here, some men, not all men, if you could even use that label to describe the type of male species that would have walked away. And, yes, I have just judged someone, and that is never a good thing.

Sometimes when Emily meets a man, he will extend a hand and expect her to shake it. She does of course—and it's awkward to explain why when you're trying to flirt. Because she feels it's more of a pity statement than a genuine greeting like a kiss on the cheek or a hug.

As we talked, which was easy, given Emily had such a gentle nature, she stopped me.

'Are you still here because you want my story, or you actually like talking to me?' she asked.

'Both,' I replied. And we carried on.

No other reply would have been valid in all honesty. I began to understand why some men would not have agreed for a date with her, had she informed them beforehand of her disability. The shock of meeting someone that does not meet your perceived expectations can be hard to face. So, I had a question I wanted to ask Emily. But for now, that question could wait.

Emily had broken her back, falling from a horse four years prior. As such she was now reliant on a wheelchair. In every other physical sense, she was functioning.

'It's a challenge in the world of dating, where even the subtlest gestures can carry a lot of intention. I simply can't do certain things,' she said.

For Emily, the worst part about not having the use of her legs, is knowing that many people don't see her as a prospective romantic partner to date, to marry, and to have children with someday. Still, she loves Singapore's night life and the possibilities that come with being in a crowd of strangers. On a recent night out, she shared that she had to manoeuvre her wheelchair to greet friends as they arrived. Since she was feeling too short, she had to raise her body up with her arms to try and be at the same height as them.

'If I ever meet the pope, I would ask him to pray that I find love,' she says with a sad smile.

I must admit I almost shed a tear at this point.

It makes you think though—dating is an emotionally risky proposition for anyone, but it is especially challenging for people with disabilities. People who rely on wheelchairs or who have another form of physical impairment often begin to date much later in life. Also, according to research by Dr Margaret Nosek, director of the Center for Research on Women with Disabilities at Baylor College of Medicine, the rate of marriage among such people is significantly lower than the average.

In many ways, young women with disabilities like Emily are just like other women their age when it comes to dating. They like dance clubs and meeting new people, and some even participate in casual hook-ups, common among young people today. But women with disabilities can also be more vulnerable. Physically not being able to walk, run, undertake certain sporting activities, and in the event of an emergency, they can't help or protect themselves.

'So, Emily, I have a question for you?'

'Sure, shoot.'

'When you match with someone online, do you tell them you have a disability?'

Emily cracked a small smile. 'No, I don't'

'Can I ask why?' It needed to be asked.

'Because. Because, I don't want to be judged.'

I pondered her response for a moment. I pondered because her reasoning made sense, but also it made no sense given the eventual outcome would be the same. Someone would either accept Emily's disability or not. The difference being the decision could be made without them having to be physically present and as such avoid any awkward situation that might ensue.

I put this thought to Emily. She understood the logic of my challenge but also hoped that deep down someone would look past her disability having met her in person and give her a chance.

I could relate to this as I was taken in by her easy nature and infectious smile and could see why her hope for a man to accept after meeting her with no prior knowledge of her condition was not so crazy after all.

I asked Emily to share next her last online dating experience.

This is what she shared.

Emily had matched with a man in his mid-thirties. He had a professional job, at least his profile had stated as much. He was an American-born Chinese, but had lived in Singapore for the past five years. She referred to him as Joe. She then commented that she had been drawn to his deep brown eyes, not his overall physical appearance. She then flashed a picture of him on her iPhone. I would describe him as neutral looking, pan faced with perhaps a little too much chub. His fashion sense had Zara written all over it, but perhaps he needed to go up a size or two to better show his potential. Not that it mattered. Emily liked him and that was all that mattered.

They had agreed to meet in Botanical Gardens, given it was a nice sunny. Emily reached the venue in good time and wheeled herself a few hundred yards from the lake. She considered the spot romantic. Lily pads the size of dinner plates to gaze upon, the occasional waft of a floral scent in the air. It was perfect. Emily had even taken charge and brought with her a bottle of wine in a cool bag and two plastic glasses.

'My wheelchair sometimes has advantages.' She proclaimed rather proudly.

Emily recalled that Joe appeared on the small hill just off to her left, almost on time. He had approached her with a lost look on this face.

'Excuse me,' Joe asked. 'Is there another lake near here?'

Emily explained to me that at this point that she knew exactly what would happen next.

'Are you Joe?' She asked.

'Yes, how . . .' Joe apparently stopped mid-sentence.

Emily then explained that the colour had drained from his face. That he had just stood there for a moment. Joe then made a statement that she had heard before.

'You're in a wheelchair.' Joe stated. Clearly an observant man. Sorry, had to slide that sarcastic comment in. I mean, really Joe?

Emily recalled that he stayed five minutes—the normal time before most men walked away—having tried to bumble some words about the fact that he was a busy guy and would not be able to take care of her. Emily laughed at this point and confirmed that all she wanted was a date, not a full-time caregiver.

'So, did this happen again?' I had to ask.

'It's happened to me a dozen or so times, but three weeks ago something else happened,' she said with an almost dead-pan face.

I, of course, wanted to know what had transpired. So, I ordered another pot of tea and settled in to hear her next encounter.

It was a Sunday, a wet Sunday, but Emily desperately needed to get outdoors for some fresh air. She loved bars and clubs, which is where most people tend to choose to meet for first dates—I know I did, but Emily was different. She decided meet Robert, an Englishman she had matched with on Tinder, at the Marina Bay Gardens. For those not familiar with Singapore, Marina Bay Gardens is a lush tropical paradise, showcasing plants and flowers from the far-flung corners of the world. Orchids, dragon fruit plants, and wild roses—it was possible to see all these here, in addition to the giant fake steel trees that stand in the middle of the gardens. They look like they belong on the movie set of Avatar.

Emily loved this place. Parked just a few yards from the main arrival entrance, right underneath one of the giant tree structures, she waited with her the statutory bottle of wine and two glasses. Emily, you could say, was a hopeless romantic and I give her full credit for trying to impress her date, which I think is a wonderful thing.

Emily had spotted Robert as he stepped out of a taxi and started to walk towards the agreed meeting point. His floppy blonde hair almost covered his face, which he brushed back as he approached. At this point, Emily paused, and I wrongly assumed she would then tell me a repeat of the first encounter she had shared. But I was wrong. Emily beamed at me and almost over-excitedly told me that he bounded right up to her and simply asked 'Hi, are you Emily?'

'My mouth almost fell open,' she said.

'Rather than look lost, or stumble his words, he just assumed it was me and said cool, after I had confirmed it was me.'

I almost cheered at this point in the story.

Emily went on. She explained that he just looked at her as a real person and asked if we could visit the 'Mountain dome.' The mountain dome is a rainforest simulation set inside a huge class greenhouse, complete with waterfall. It also caters fully for people in wheelchairs. Much to Emily's joy he didn't try too hard and insist on pushing her, he just walked beside her.

'He was so funny.' She explained.

'He would challenge me to a race up one of the ramps, which of course he won, but it put me at ease.'

'He also asked what happened if I ever got a flat tire.'

As I listened to her, I could see how happy she was. It was as simple as someone just accepting that she was in every way a beautiful woman. Her disability did not detract from her own character, and in many ways perhaps made her all the more appealing. She had met someone that looked beyond her disability and just accepted it from the get go.

The date ended with the two of them drinking the wine, sharing a kiss, and agreeing to see each other again. Robert had struck gold, and it seemed Emily had too. Robert never looked or treated her any differently to someone who was able-bodied, aside the obvious help now and then. They have been dating ever since. At this point, I gave her a hug and told her to invite me to the wedding, should one ever loom on the horizon. Just as I did, Robert arrived to meet her. I shook his hand, thanked them both and left them to it. It is my wish they find happiness. Two such people deserve it. It just goes to show, never give up hope.

BONUS SWIPE 4

Classic Love Versus Tinder

If there's one thing we all enjoy, it's a great love story. One that fills our hearts with the joy, hope, and sometimes even despair and reveals the power of human attraction. We also often look for a story that inspires us with wonderful characters and a gripping plot—one that we'll read time and again, just to inhabit the world the author has created for us.

But how do you choose the best from the worst? It's impossible to do so, but that hasn't stopped us trying. So, without further ado, sit back and enjoy my guide to the best love stories ever told. But wait, I have added a twist. What if Tinder, or other such applications, was available when these love stories were written.

William Shakespeare's *Romeo and Juliet*. No question, that this is a real classic, even if it's a bit overdone nowadays. It's been made into a play, a film, and produced for TV. But that doesn't detract from the ability of Shakespeare's heart-breaking tale to tell us all we need to know about human longing. Sit before the star-crossed heroes at the play's end, their arms entwined in a deathly embrace, and you see with utter clarity that true love is impossible to control. Then wipe your eyes, blow your nose and return to daily life, knowing that nothing will ever be the same again. This is without question one of the best love stories ever written—with a quill pen or otherwise.

But what if a mobile dating app was available then? Having Romeo send a text message saying 'Yet tell me not, for I have heard it all. Here's much to do with hate, but more with love.' It would just seem weird and most likely end with the receiver deleting the sender within seconds. So, what has changed? Our love language for sure has changed. That same message today would probably be something like 'Don't banter on, I love you.'

In the original play, Romeo makes his first appearance a few moments after the prince has ended a fight between Montagues and Capulets. These lines establish that Romeo is tired of the feud between the two families. He compares the families' hatred to his own love for Rosaline, which establishes the close connection between love and violence running throughout the play.

'I fear too early, for my mind misgives;
Some consequence, yet hanging in the stars,
Shall bitterly begin.'

Was everything that bad back then, so tragic? In today's context, you would simply not have that situation, but it does demonstrate that we convey everything through text now, rather than a conversation. Does this make a situation worse or easier in the context of a feud or disagreement between two people? One thing is for sure, if Romeo was on Tinder, his messages would take some understanding, so while language has changed, we also now have a social language that sometimes we do not understand even now. We live in a world of abbreviations and emoticons.

'Want to see me tonight bro? LOL. No ONS or hook-up, okay lah.'

I wonder what Shakespeare would make of that. Perhaps:

'Yee step out upon the stars, for no harm will befall you.'

The writer of *Anna Karenina*, Leo Tolstoy—also known as Count Nikolayevich Tolstoy—was probably one of the greatest authors of all time. *Anna Karenina* is set against the panoramic backdrop of nineteenth-century Russia. Tolstoy's tale operates at many levels. At its heart is the adulterous relationship between the title character and the dashing Count Vronsky. Not to spoil the story for those that have not read the book, but it doesn't end well, with Anna throwing herself in front of a moving train and her suicidal lover heading off on a death mission to fight the Turks. But there's a parallel romance for those who like their love stories less tragic: Anna's sister-in-law's sister Kitty eventually falls in love and marries the likeable Levin, who himself undergoes a journey of self-discovery that many critics regard as Tolstoy's real purpose for writing Anna Karenina.

Relating this to today's dating scene, adultery is common place. Married men, women, and even couples now seek additional marital fun. So, we ask ourselves if technology and the ease with which it can be used as a social bee hive had propagated this trend. I myself had multiple offers to *swing* or become a third leg in a marriage. I said no for the avoidance of doubt. But truth is, temptation is all around us.

One lady I met, while researching this book, who shall remain nameless, found herself embroiled in such a situation.

The man she had matched with on Tinder was married, but this was not known to her at the time of her agreeing to meet him. He certainly did not declare this in his profile. Some do, which while odd, at least, is honest.

'Married. Just wanting some discreet fun' is a profile tag I have seen a dozen times. Nothing out of the ordinary I hear you say. It happens all the time. But consider this. She met this man multiple times over the course of six months. No suspicion was raised as the man she met seemed genuine, met her when planned, and seemed at ease in public. All seemed well. This is until messages started to land on her phone. The wife had gotten hold of her number and started to send accusations. The penny dropped, and the decision to confront the wayward husband was made. Just like Anna Karenina, it did not end well. No trains were jumped in front of, but the poor wife of the man that betrayed her did self-harm in a cry for help. This is in any situation a tragic outcome. They say that once a person cheats on another, in the context of a relationship, they will always cheat, no matter how much they promise not to do so again.

Best advice I can offer—do not get involved with a married man or woman. It never ends well.

In *Wuthering Heights* by Emily Bronte, which I must add is one of my all-time favourites, have you noticed the link between love and anguish? No one understood this better than Emily Bronte in my opinion, whose one and only novel is an absolute knockout. Heathcliff loves Cathy, and Cathy loves Heathcliff. But as with all good Victorian novels, class status and snobbery gets in the way of their passion. To cut a long story short, pretty much every character in the book ends up bitter, twisted, and heartbroken. Not much has changed to this day. But love never dies, and that's what makes this a story to be reckoned with.

Putting this story into today's context, I would like to focus on the class and snobbery aspect. Cathy and Heathcliff faced it then, and I believe that it still exists today. When we match with someone on a dating app, we don't know much about someone's background. This is in the first instance established via chatting over text messages. We all come from different backgrounds and some of the people we meet come from less privileged or minority backgrounds from where they might have risen to become well-standing and successful people in society. But how accepting are we really when we meet someone for the first time? We all shop with our eyes first, so the profile match is made largely upon physical appearance or the profile introduction written by some. I'm still surprised at how many people don't write one.

Elizabeth, a British lady of fair stature and in her thirties, originally from Nigeria encountered snobbery and class distinction of the worst kind. It wasn't racism, more a series of shallow judgements against her background when dating men.

Elizabeth's parents had been a hardworking couple and upon immigration to the UK, set about building a new life together away from the tyranny and fear of living in Nigeria. They settled in what is known as 'Little Lagos' Peckham in South London. Her father worked in construction while her mother cleaned houses, took in laundry, and upon Elizabeth's birth, took care of her and continued her work with Elizabeth in tow at time. She always had food in her stomach and a roof over her head. Her family were simple loving people going about their lives. Despite having been schooled in the public system, Elizabeth graduated with a degree in law and went on to become a successful corporate lawyer. That is itself is to be admired.

Being single was not on her long-term agenda as she wanted a family of her own. Thus, her search for a suitable partner began, and she soon found herself using online dating apps. After a few dates, she began to realize that the men she was dating, most of whom were also professionals, judged her on her background. She had openly shared her history with pride. Elizabeth, found she was having to explain what she felt men needed to understand about Nigerian women. This is what she shared with me.

Dating Nigerian women can be tricky for any man, but especially for those with a different nationality, and Elizabeth had a strong connection to her roots as conditioned by her parents. Given that she was born and raised in the UK, this meant she mostly dated British men. Elizabeth shared that based on whether one is talking to a conservative, traditional Nigerian woman or a more modern, open-minded one, there are a couple of things to keep in mind.

Work and occupation matter to Nigerian women, and they are very likely to ask about what you do for a living on the first date. Although some people may refer to them as gold-diggers, this just has to do with their culture and how they want a man who can provide for a family. Elizabeth laughed at this point at the thought of her being seen as a gold-digger, given she was a lawyer and considered herself to be financially stable.

However, Nigerian women are also hard-workers who are willing and wanting to do their part to contribute to the financial aspect of a relationship, which is why they see laziness as a turn-off. Elizabeth wants to see that a man has goals and ambitions.

Elizabeth then points out that Nigerian women are also unlikely to marry a foreigner. Because of their traditional, religious background, it is difficult for Nigerian women to relate to men from other sides of the world, and even harder to get them to the aisle if they are conservative. We African women happen to be extremely close to our family and friends. Therefore, most of them are more than happy to stay in their country, and would prefer a partner who would be comfortable with relocating to Nigeria eventually. However, given that Elizabeth was born in the UK, she was open to dating non-Nigerian men.

Nigerian women, like many women from other countries, are into the little details. Flowers, chocolate, cards, and old-fashioned romantic gestures will get you way further with a Nigerian beauty than intense talking. Nigerian girls she points out want to feel special, treasured, and loved, but are also shy in public, so the perfect way to show them how much you care is with gifts that reflect their personality, rather than making out on the streets. By the way, always ask first before you try to kiss them or get closer.

Elizabeth then reflected on her own experiences. She had met a total of six men, none of whom bought her flowers or show any level of respect. Most of these six made her feel as if she was below them in class and status, given that her parents came from a country they considered third world. One man she recalled even corrected her on the usage of cutlery when out for dinner. 'He had the nerve to inform me that I was using the wrong fork, followed by stating I had clearly gone to the wrong school!' recounted Elizabeth.

She went on. What these men missed out on learning is that Nigerian women are great in the kitchen. They are taught very early in life how to cook amazing dishes, a skill that they improve over the years by adding more international flavours to their recipes. In fact, if you date a Nigerian girl, not only will you never starve, you'll be more than pleased with the way they cook for you, your friends, and your family. 'We can manage an entire buffet and still make everything delicious, guaranteed!' she said laughing. 'But, every once in a while, we are also happy for you to cook for us.'

Elizabeth then blushed as she shared how Nigerian women are also adventurous in the bedroom. Though some people refer to Nigerian ladies as being submissive, they are always willing to go the extra mile to satisfy their men, which definitely includes sex. If you are certain that they care about you, don't be afraid to tell them about your ideas on how to spice things up and step out of the box, you'd be surprised with how against the norm they can go when they love someone.

Elizabeth ends by saying that her search continues to find a man who will love her. She has much to offer but asks, don't judge her on how to use a fork—she knows. And if you are a snob, pass her by. What a wonderful lady.

Pride and Prejudice by Jane Austen. Talking of snobbery, Austen's deceptively comedic tale of Georgian manners is a masterclass in social commentary. But, at its heart is a good old-fashioned love story, rather a few of them. The most striking one is, of course, between Elizabeth Bennet and Mr Darcy, whose relationship is established along the now-standard lines of initial coldness, mutual attraction, large-misunderstanding-that-leads-to-more-coldness, and eventual happily-ever-after-union. Perhaps, a few men on Tinder should place this book on their must-read list, because to me, it demonstrates that arrogance in ego have no place in relationships and personal barriers must be let down.

BONUS SWIPE 5

Shock Factor

'I love a brilliant man,' Karen conveyed to me. I had, in fact, barely taken a seat.

'Great. We will get along fine then,' I added with tongue in cheek.

This story is about Karen, a lady in her late forties. She is a marketing executive with the class of a Krug bottle of champagne.

'I study men to better understand what makes them intelligent. If you're an intelligent man who I consider is smarter than most of the men I meet, I would assume it can be frustrating to realize that other guys with far less brain power than them seem to be fighting women off with a stick. So, what gives? Why isn't their intelligence giving them a clear advantage when it comes to women?'

It is partly for this reason that Karen loved to be around men she considered smart.

'But how best to describe Tom? A handsome Englishman in his early thirties, of tall and refined stature who looked like he had fallen out of an Alfred Dunhill catalogue. Was it his high-flying career in banking? Or, was it the fact he could talk in-depth about almost anything on the planet? No, brilliant men are everywhere. But Tom had the ability to re-energize himself by taking moments to reflect on where he was heading in life, and change course when he needed to. He believed in fail fast, learn fast. He was a humble man for a banker, which is rare, and able to look deep within himself. I say this because he was one of the rare men I have met, especially via a dating app that took responsibility for his own life and marriage failure. Not because of a sordid affair, but his career had taken up far too much of his focus and time.'

'Tom took the time to learn from his mistakes and embraced humility. So, you couldn't judge Tom's brilliance by his career success, or by how much money he made, or by how many houses and pieces or artworks by famous abstract painters he owned. Tom was brilliant because he could judge himself and fix his behaviour according to the situation at hand. Tom had absolute objectivity. How could such a man not have been snapped up by any woman who would respect such attributes? Was he superman and worthy of wearing his underpants outside of his trousers? I think so.'

'I pondered on this point more than once. Our introductory texts got deep very quickly, and Tom was not afraid to describe his love of sex or talking about the women that had journeyed thorough his past since his very bitter divorce. The women as he described, ranged from total tarts, weirdos, fetish freaks, earth lovers, women's rights activists to highly successful businesswomen. But none of them seemed to have lasted beyond three months. By his own admission, he was a workaholic and travelled incessantly in his spare time. This I suspected was the issue and the root cause of his divorce. Tom could be described very accurately as, handsome by anyone's standards and extremely strong of character.'

Karen recalls having seen Tom three or four times since their match on Tinder for drinks, dinners, and a casual coffee here and there, before she was invited over for supper one evening, to his home. This is how she remembers it.

'The intimacy between us was moving to the next level. Upon arrival at his luxury penthouse condo, I took a moment to calm myself and buzzed the intercom.'

I interjected here and asked her to explain why she needed to calm herself?

'The last time I had buzzed an intercom was while on a blind date. A friend of mine had invited me to one of his friend's dinner parties and she was to be my blind date, in addition to her being the host. The intercom was the kind that had a camera and a miniature screen on which I could see the host's face. The seventy-year old, somewhat prune like face that greeted me, almost turned me to stone. What's the mythical Greek lady with hair of snakes? Yes, her. Luckily, it was the wrong apartment and the mystery was solved.'

'So, I steadied my nerves and was buzzed up to Tom's penthouse. All was well as Tom greeted me with a kiss and a bunch of flowers. Now this was five-star treatment I had never encountered before. Luckily for me I had brought with me a gift of fine wine, such were my own manners upon arriving at someone's home. I add here that a good bottle of wine says much about the person's class distinction and taste. Whereas a cheap bottle of wine means cheap, can't be bothered, or just plain old tight.

Tom kissed me on both cheeks, being European, and thanked me for the wine and zoomed off to the kitchen to fix me a drink. It was an open plan kitchen, so I could see him as he chatted on and skilfully removed the cork from a champagne bottle—and no, not with his teeth or the edge of a sword.'

'Meanwhile, I was scanning the living room. His apartment had more candles than a catholic church. The walls were covered with black and white photographs, oils, and other such forms of art, which dripped from every square inch of the wall's. Stark white sofas configured in an L-shape faced a sixty-inch flat screen TV. A large dining table that the twelve apostles would struggle to fill and a fluffy rug took centre stage in the vast openplan dining area. It strangely had a very feminine touch, with strokes of masculinity. I wondered how much of the style was a leftover from his former wife. But that would be rude to ask.'

'His entire penthouse and duplex apartment screamed high-end design and items of quality. I felt a little bit like I was in the Getty museum in Los Angeles. Stone statues seemed to eye you up from every corner of the room!'

'Tom took a seat next to me on the sofa. I kicked off my shoes as he handed me a glass of bubbles. Tom put his feet up and sipped the champagne while looking at me intently. This was followed by a loving stroke to the arm, as if to pet me like a cat and give me a sign that he was feeling comfortable, happy, and a little intimate. With the touch of a button on some high-tech device, music calmly filled the air and added to the building mood. Everything seemed perfect.

'Tom then got up and returned to the kitchen and prompted me to talk about my life. Small talk was now underway. I had no issue with this and recounted my career, divorce, and various hobbies. I added in the fact I had just returned from London and enjoyed every moment of my trip—seeing Buckingham Palace, visiting the museums, and lunch at Harrods.'

'Tom listened intently with the occasional sigh to let me know he was listening and put together a cheese and cold meat platter fit for a king, or queen, and returned to the sofa. I was being very well looked after.'

'With another flick of the high-tech remote, the lights dimmed and the music changed. A track from Annie Lennox if I recall. It was all getting very comfortable. We kissed, then kissed again, passionately.

'We chatted a little about his kids and his former wife. The conversation was refreshing in that he was complimentary about her despite the bitterness and stated that life just went its separate ways. He did, however, mention that he supported her still. This was a topic I stayed neutral on. But I did wonder why. But, at least for now, it was none of my business. I reminded myself never to judge or comment on an ex-partner in the early stages of your relationship. It only serves to backfire at some stage. Listen, but stay silent. I had experienced far too many dates where the topic of conversation was all about an ex-wife, and it serves no purpose in the early days. I had been used too many times as someone's punch back or venting source. Never again.'

'We picked at the cheese, cold meat, and dried fruit. The music played on and he inched closer, entwining an arm and toasting to us and our future with the champagne, which endlessly seemed to flow from a large wine fridge in the kitchen. This was followed by more petting and more kissing. I, at this point inched away, as I could tell where this was heading. I was being seduced, and he may as well have announced it. A woman knows the signs, and I wasn't at all sure if I was ready. The next time he went to kiss me I manoeuvred a slice of salami into his mouth. It worked for a while at least.'

'After hour or so, he became more passionate and off came his garments one by one. First, his socks, then his shirt, and then his jeans. I wasn't aware we were playing strip poker, and I asked him what he was doing. Getting comfortable he said. I had a decision to make and it wasn't as if he was not handsome and sexy. So, inhibited by the champagne, I cast caution to the wind. I too started to shed some items of clothing.'

'Before long we were both as naked as the day we were born. The kissing continued and Tom somehow managed to extend his arm around me, as I was now on top of him. This is when it happened. He leaned in and bit down hard on one of my nipples. To say I screamed like a woman being murdered by Jack the Ripper would be an understatement. I leapt up, at least it felt that way, three feet in the air and ran around to the back of the sofa. I was in total shock.'

'What the blue blazes was that? I recall shouting and rubbing my now sore nipple.'

'Tom sat up and looked at me as if I had landed from the moon. He had this look on his face, like he had been slapped across the face with a wet fish.'

'I just love it he said. Such a turn on. Is there a problem? He said cool as ice.'

I had to ask Karen at this point, what happened next?

She shared with me that Tom dressed, apologized, and asked for a start over. She had explained to Tom that night that it wasn't her thing at all so soon into knowing someone. Tom then made the mistake of digging the hole he was in even deeper by informing Karen that biting her nipples was a must for him and he considered that Karen would grow to like it too. Karen conveyed that Tom then went to great details about how it would have enhanced their lovemaking experience and mentioned how he would follow it up next time with a finger into a sensitive opening.

I will pause writing this story here for a moment. Because, I have never seen the blood drain from a lady's face as fast as Karen's as she clearly remembered the incident as if it had happened just a few moments ago. It was as if someone had pulled a drain plug in her lower back and allowed every bit of liquid to flow out.

She had remembered feeling sick and almost thrown up the cold meat and grapes she had eaten before. After a few minutes and a strong cup of tea, Karen continued. She explained how Tom believed that such an act would enhance his erection.

Needless to say, Karen gathered up her clothes, confirmed that no, she would not wish to be a party to enhancing his erection further and left.

In the taxi journey home, Karen tried to rationalize what had happened.

I must interject here. Have you noticed how many of us reflect on experiences like this on the journey home? I guess it is just human nature to do so and try to regain control. Back to Karen, she couldn't reconcile with what had just happened. She put it down to feeling invaded; there was no gentle lead up, just an attack. It honestly felt to her like an attack. She knew, of course, it wasn't, but Tom's approach had simply been wrong. Either way, it was not something she was willing to accept on the first lovemaking date. That was that. Ironically, they did stay in touch for a while. Karen concludes that it wasn't that they disliked each other, they simply had different views on acceptable foreplay.

BONUS SWIPE 6

When One Is Not Enough

I'm sure, that like me, you've may have reached a point in one relationship—at least one that started because of a Tinder swipe—when you wanted to get away from Tinder and promise never to return again. You may have felt that things were going well enough and that there was no need to keep searching for other people since you were happy with the person you were with. Of course, this is likely to depend on the stage you are at in the newfound relationship. Many people continue to swipe and date multiple people. As long as that expectation is set, no harm done.

At least this is how I had felt in the past and how Caroline felt when she was into her four-month anniversary with Barry. She had travelled to exotic destinations and bathed in the sun. Sailed yachts over coral reefs and sipped wine in enchanting bars. She had spent weekends chilling out at her home watching television reruns of *House of Cards*. She had hit the town, danced, and enjoyed several romantic dinners. And, all this, with him. Barry had become more than just a man to date, he had become special. They had, of course, also enjoyed a physical relationship, and it was one that had brought them both even closer.

The term 'date' is used in the courtship sense here, to mean that two people with a romantic inclination towards each other agree to meet on a given day at an agreed time. Where you meet and what you both do together when you meet is a matter of personal choice. These dates can be repeated or not, until you reach a stage which some call a relationship, a point in time when you both feel more committed to each other. You feel safe, secure, and fulfilled. To not be with that person would present a void in your life. I guess it can also be called love.

There is also a general understanding that such relationships are, or should be, exclusive. You are not in need of seeing anyone else with regard to romance and love. Love can be blind they say—not that Caroline was at a stage ready to utter those words to Barry, but she was extremely fond of him.

Caroline assumed that given Barry always made time for her and the fact that his willingness to meet with her never faltered, he had the same level of feeling and commitment to her as she did to him. But as the saying goes, assumption can be the mother of all screw-ups. It is so very true from my own experience!

When I enquired further with Caroline about her views on making assumptions and if she had made any wrong ones, she shared this encounter.

'I was once on an airplane to Bali where I spent the entire four hours sitting next to and talking to a guy who said he was a professional footballer. We talked about love, religion, and dreams. After the flight, we exchanged contact details, and I absolutely wanted to stay in touch with him. Over the course of two weeks and having spent my entire Bali vacation with him, I began to fantasize about a life together. It was a crazy notion to have, but that is how I felt at the time. It went as far as me thinking what our wedding would be like? What would our children look like? Where would we live?'

'Okay, okay, I got a bit carried away, but he was the first man I could see a future with since my last breakup. The truth is, we all do it to some degree.'

'We all tend fantasize about people we are particularly attracted to. When we meet them or even just see them from afar, we make judgements about what they must be like, wonder about their lives, find their Instagram and Facebook for visual aids, and then we use those visual aids, assumptions, and our own romantic ideals to imagine what life would be like with this person in it. The human mind is the perfect incubator for an ideal partner. Sometimes we forget they are just a figment of our imagination. We project this fantasy onto the person in front of us who *looks* like our new imaginary friend.'

'If you think it's worthwhile to turn fantasy into reality, and you have the courage to actually reach out to this person, well, you won't exactly have an unbiased first date. Since you've already imagined a beautiful life, say, in Bali or Europe with a really big family and an endless bucket list, anything they say on the date that contradicts this fantasy is a threat to your potential relationship. Therefore, you try to rationalize, forgive, and stretch the reality so that maybe things will change, the person will change, and your fantasy can come true. This is *not healthy*.'

'Our brain uses heuristics to make sense of the world around us without having to interact with it, and it can be strongly influenced by what we are feeling in the moment. Heuristics are mental shortcuts that cause us to make immediate judgement decisions based on information we have previously learned about people and processed, stereotypes, and the way the world works. These heuristics go haywire when browsing through social media or only taking small bits of information from a conversation without fully listening and communicating. You see what you want to see and hear what you want to hear.'

'Ultimately, these heuristics cause us to make cognitive biases such as the halo effect and confirmation bias. Using the halo effect, we take every unattractive thing someone we are interested in says or does and spin it in a positive thought or action, because this person is attractive and therefore must be an angel, especially since we've already pictured getting married to them and having a big family. After fantasizing, we steer the conversation in a way that confirms our preconceived notions and assumptions, and then we only remember the info that validates our fantasy. That's the confirmation bias.'

'Basically, our brains are processing all these things for you, and it continues to jump to conclusions in order to make our life easier and better. But we can train it to jump to a better conclusion—one that always says we'll know more if we ask, and a healthier fantasy, one of you two, on a first date, getting to know each other without any preconceived ideas that you expect the other to live up to.'

'In short, you can tell your brain that you want to start getting to know people the hard way by not giving it any information to fantasize over. It is essential not to fantasize too much. Do not make assumptions of where and what you think the relationship will become. And above all, don't stalk their social media. Don't ask friends for information. Let them tell you their story themselves—that way, when you listen, you will actually listen. You will not only be able to listen to them better, but you can listen to your instincts much better because you're not trying to prove to yourself that this is the one. If you already went on a date and still find yourself fantasizing—kind of like me in this experience, and I should have considered the airplane journey my date. It just means that you really do like this person. That's beautiful! Just make sure to take it one step at a time. I should have thought about a real date first rather than a marriage!'

'Also, don't assume that just because you know enough to have real feelings for someone that you actually know them. In fact, this is even more unhealthy than making assumptions about someone you don't know and have no intention of talking to again. When you assume things about someone you are actually dating or intending to date, they are affected by your judgements, too. They will be able to feel that you are looking at them through a certain lens, and it can make them feel very uneasy and misunderstood. I've been there. I have had a former boyfriend expecting me to be always joyful—the happy girl that I appeared to be. And I could feel his disappointment every time he realized that I was not actually that girl. It broke my heart each time, I couldn't live up to his fantasy of me.'

'Save yourselves the drama. Make every effort to not assume anything about a person and bother to take the time to find out. The only conclusion you should be jumping to is that the only way to truly get to know someone is by communicating better, in real life, not in your imagination! Ask questions, listen to answers, and if something confuses you or rubs you the wrong way, don't make excuses for them! It's not fair to yourself or your partner to pretend they meant something else. So, next time you catch yourself assuming things, remember: 'I'll know more if I ask!'

'In the end, the footballer and I broke up and that was that.'

'If only I had remembered that when I was dating Barry. Why you ask? This is why. My friend Jane was surfing Tinder over lunch one Sunday when she came across a profile, read the short blurb of the guy and swiped right. She later explained that they had matched and had engaged in some banter.'

She said that the guy, who went by the name of John, was flirtatious, cheeky, and fun. She had no idea if that was his real name, given that 40 per cent of the men she had swiped on all carried that name. Over the course of a few weeks she kept me informed of his antics, the dates she had, and other more personal fun facts. 'Not that we girls talk about the Tinder men we date all of the time in such graphic detail!'

'Meanwhile, I was dating Barry and things were going really well. I wanted the same having been single for a while. Strangely by coincidence, it must have been hunting season on Tinder because another friend, Joanne, had also matched with a guy named Ken, and she too was having a lot of fun.'

'After a week or so, we all met for lunch again, confirmed that we were all still dating and decided the three of us should all meet up as couples. Now, this for a lady, is a big step. Introducing your newfound love to your friends means something. Either that you want their opinion or their blessing. We all agreed, and a date and place was agreed and set. In hindsight, this had been a bad idea. I go back to my story earlier about assumptions and the guy I met in Bali. I had built a fantasy that we would all meet, love each other, and have a wonderful time. I didn't know then that we would not, but I had again allowed myself to set expectations.'

'Barry had gone off to play football and consume far too many beers with his friends on the morning of the lunch and agreed to meet me there later. Jane and Joanne, as always, would need a reminder so I pinged off a message to say that I was on my way. I assumed, of course, that they both could still make it and that they would have their new loves in tow. I'm always the organized one, in case you were wondering, and it's for good reason that I mention it.

I had downed my first glass of wine by the time Jane arrived with her man. But it wasn't the guy she was expecting to bring as he had called in sick with a bout of 'man flu'. For those of you who have not heard of this illness, and I believe it has even now found a place in the Oxford Dictionary. Man-flu is when a man claims to have a cold or other such illness, but over exaggerates the effects and makes it seem worse than it actually is. Sometimes they are not ill at all. Anyway, the guy now with Jane, and he looked like he needed a shot of penicillin himself, was an emergency pick-up date. I had to give her credit for finding someone at the last minute, but it kind of killed the point of the couples' lunch. Even more surprising was the fact Jane introduced this poor man as her stand-in date. He didn't seem to care of mind as he took a seat and started to play with his phone. Probably swiping on Tinder.'

'Joanne then arrived, but alone. Where's your man? I enquired. Somewhat ashamed Joanne shared that he had double-booked and necked back the remains of my glass of wine. Needless to say, we ordered a few bottles after that. The couple's lunch I had assumed would be perfect, was turning into a not so couples' lunch and yet again assumption was proven wrong, or is it right?'

'After forty or so minutes, I was growing concerned that Barry was a no show, so I called him, given no messages had come in. He eventually replied stating that she was tired from football, had devoured way too many beers and needed to sleep it off. This was the trigger to finally turn the lunch into a joke. I didn't argue, made apologies for him and we all concluded lunch. Despite the now awkward aspect of us all now having dinner with one man, Mr Emergency Date, he was actually okay, and Jane seemed happy. At least she had a stand-in. Then again why would Mr Emergency Date guy not also be happy about having lunch with three awesome women.'

'Later that evening, something was bothering me. Something didn't seem right. Barry had never cancelled on me and it was unlikely that he would use football as a viable excuse. So, I called him again as I needed an explanation. Sadly, I reached his voice mail asking me in an overly happy voice to leave a message. Same thing an hour later. I finally got in touch with him the next morning and asked if he was okay. He explained that he was and why was I so concerned. I accepted his confirmation that he was just tired, had slept early, and it was a plausible reason. We met each other a few days later for drinks. Barry seemed to be himself and all was good. That is until a mutual friend of Jane's had decided to invite us all to a barbeque that approaching weekend. The sausages, beer, wine, and chunky beef burgers had been purchased, and we again thought about how nice it would be for the ladies and the men to all meet as couples. Only this time I kept my assumptions in check. I confirmed with Jane and Joanne that they were still with the same men and no emergency date would appear on scene. Call me paranoid, but I did ask, given a week was the average duration of their respective dates staying the course—not that I had set any world records myself.'

'Beer and wine were flowing, and the smell of sizzling steak and sausages filled the air. People were mingling, chatting, and flirting away. People were having fun. Thankfully for Jane, Joanne, and I, there wasn't an emergency date in sight. At least not between us, but a couple standing near us could possibly qualify. You can tell if a couple are new or having trouble. The man definitely seemed awkward. Meanwhile, the woman was model quality. We all wondered why she was standing with the male equivalent of Mr Bean. People watching is such great fun, isn't it!'

'We each shyly checked our phones. It seemed like we had all been ditched again in place of a feeble excuse. We compared notes—Jane's boyfriend had been hit with a family emergency and Joanne's other half had a case of food poisoning. We all laughed it off—that is, until Jane pointed out the blindingly obvious. So obvious to us now, it stood out like tits on a bull!

Perhaps we should all have known better. It was a fact so simple that we all felt like complete idiots. It is that moment in life when the lightbulb goes off, and you wonder how you could have been so dumb. What is the one thing most women, and even guys for that matter, do? They proudly flash a picture of their girlfriend or boyfriend to their mates, to showboat, and to boost their pride. For some reason, we hadn't done so.'

'So, just like that, because we wanted to reveal the man who had abandoned us at that barbeque, which wasn't so bad since we had food and wine, we selected our favourite pictures on our phones and showed them to each other. One at a time. At that precise moment in time, it felt as though the earth beneath my feet had opened up and I had fallen into a deep black hole. I swear my mouth had dropped open and drool was dripping out. Jane and Joanne were looking at me as if I were a ghost. The second feeling I had before a wave of anger took over was as if a knife had been driven into my guts, twisting, and pulling out repeatedly, and with each thrust, my pride had been torn into shreds.'

'Both Jane and Joanne were now turning in circles, looking at their phones, then at me, then back at their phones. They were both trying to speak but no words were coming out. Jane spoke fist after a few minutes.'

'"No Fu#&ing way"—minus the obvious expletive in between.'

'We were all looking at the photograph of the same man. They were all pictures of Barry, or Tim, or Jim, or whatever the hell his real name was. Jane then showed her level of shock by trying to find an explanation, thinking that Barry, Jim or Tim could be triplets. The daggers we cast with our eyes back at Jane addressed that one. It was a comment which, while logical, almost lead her to be slapped by one of us!'

'It took a few days for us to gather our thoughts but we agreed not to spill the beans to Barry, Jim, and Tim—or, as he was now called, Mr Prick. We were all to stay silent and carry on as if we didn't know anything. It was a Monday, I recall, two excruciating weeks later when we finally hatched a plan. I was to bring Barry, while Jane and Joanne would meet me at a very public rooftop bar. It was one of Barry's favourite places to drink. It overlooked the Singapore river and cityscape beyond and was always bustling with couples, singles, and groups enjoying after-work drinks. I walked in with Barry at around 7 p.m., and we took a seat. Barry kissed me and asked for two G&Ts to ease the mood. I declined and ordered my favourite, a lychee martini.'

'I then drew in a deep breath and looked at Barry. I recall asking him if he would like to try something different too. Barry smiled and agreed. The waiter waited patiently for the order, and I ordered two lychee martinis. The waiter left and Barry looked at me with a puzzled expression. I waved over Jane and Joanne who had been waiting in the wings on the other side of the bar. I then informed Barry that I had two friends I wanted him to meet and I was sure he would love to know them, while trying not to lose my composure and if I'm honest, laugh. The world went into slow motion.'

'As Jane and Joanne arrived, Barry's face was priceless—a mash-up of "oh Fu#&" and a flash of trying to recover his dignity. Neither Jane or Joanne or I made a fuss, so as not to embarrass him in a social situation. We were all bigger than that. But we didn't know how he would react. So, we all looked on and waited with baited breath. For a brief moment, we thought he may pass out or have a heart attack. His face drained of blood. No, Barry simply stood up, looked at each of us in turn for what seemed like a lifetime and left without another word passing his lips.'

'We were all a little disappointed at that. We had expected some level of fireworks, rage, or attempts to pitifully explain himself out of the situation. But the player had been caught like a rat in a trap. He had not been satisfied with one of us—one was not enough for him. He wanted it all. He had lost his hand at poker, and we were all the better for it.'

'So, there you have it. I have from that day on level-checked every assumption, and never fantasized again about a man and where we may end up in the future.'

'Mr Eugene Lewis Fordsworthe once said assumption is the mother of all mistakes. He later said that his earlier philosophy of assumption being the mother of all mistakes was flawed, and he recognized that sometimes good comes from assumptions. He said that sometimes when there is not enough information, a person must make assumptions to progress. He was later quoted as saying, "I am in a bit of a paradox, for I have assumed that there is no good in assuming."

If there is not enough information but an objective need to be met quickly, then making an assumption is a good thing. Some would call that situation as "the glass is half-full".'

'As such on every date since, I have assumed the glass is half-full and may never spill over.'

BONUS SWIPE 7

The Shameless Cougar

A cougar is typically defined as an older woman who is primarily attracted to younger men, often in a sexual way. Although there is no specific age of a cougar, but the woman is usually 45 years or older with the man more than ten years her junior. Some people consider 'cougar' to be a sexist and derogatory term, but the meaning varies from offensive to empowering depending on the person and your personal point of view.

The earliest documented use for the term 'cougar' as it pertains to a woman seeking such a relationship is said to have been derived from a website in 2001 that promoted relationships between older women and younger men. The website became the focus of a story in the *Toronto Sun* when Columnist Valerie Gibson leveraged her investigations into cougardate.com to write a 2002 self-help book titled *Cougar: A Guide for Older Women Dating Younger Men*.

Hollywood is littered with Cougars. Some well-known examples come to mind immediately: Sheryl Crowe (41) and Lance Armstrong (32) in 1988, Demi Moore (48) and Ashton Kutcher (27) in 2003, Rachel Hunter (37) and Jarret Stoll (24) in 2005, and, of course, one must mention Ivana Trump (59) and Rossano Rubicondi (36) in 2008.

Now allow me to introduce you to Carol, a fifty-year-old shameless cougar by her own definition—a widow, British, and still looking as hot as a molten volcano.

Carol started by explaining that it's probably understandable that the market was flooded with erotic fiction after the success of *Fifty Shades of Grey*. In fact, thousands of e-books and straight up rip-offs of the E.L. James novel appeared and fuelled the blockbuster book revival. She had herself read *Fifty Shades of Grey* and a book called *The Cougar Diaries* by Aoife Brennan. While the former centred on the unlikely sexual adventures of two rather shallow characters, the situations in this novel are all too real. Carol wanted to read something far raunchier and more entertaining and more in-line with who she was.

Carol wanted, with the help of Tinder and a personal relationship coach she calls Leo, to get back in the saddle. Since that decision, Carol has got back on the horse and then some. Listening to her, she captures the spirit of a woman who finds herself thrust back into the dating scene after almost twenty years. Her husband of twenty years had died of cancer. Her story also speaks to any woman who feels sometimes a little confused by what men want from women. Carol believes many want mothering and security, and given she was financially secure she was okay with that. But she adds, she is no sugar mummy and not a woman to be scammed.

Carol was now very eager to tell me about one of her dates. So, I sat back, pinned back my ears and listened. I was also extremely eager to understand the world of the cougar.

Carol left work early one Friday evening and began to get herself ready. The arduous task of getting polished, preened, and prepared took a couple of hours. She made a point of saying that the older the real estate, the more maintenance you have to perform.

She had exfoliated, de-fuzzed, moisturised, and applied the usual amount of slap—makeup. She had fingered through her wardrobe pulling things out and putting them back again. She had already put on a leopard print body suit. Yes, a cougar dressed in a leopard print suit, she confessed a bit cliché, but it accentuated her curves and covered up her wobbly bits. Not that she had ever had a guy complain about her wobbly bits and most men preferred a woman with curves. But then, Carol changed her mind and selected a gold dress instead. It had a zip in the front she shamelessly explained, something very useful on certain occasions. Carol was for sure bold, old, shameless but fun.

With the dress decided, Carol sat on the bed and picked up a packet of hold-up stockings she had bought especially for the date. She unwrapped them and carefully smoothed them out. She confessed that she liked wearing them as they always had the effect of making her feel sexy and always had a powerful effect on the male of the species without exception. As she pulled them on, her mind wandered off to a memory that she kept in a box in her head. She opened the lid and allowed the memory to wash over her in all its sensuous delights.

'His hands on my body, his lips on mine, the feeling of him inside me. My whole body flushed as each part of our last steamy encounter replayed in my head.'

Her anticipation, she recounted, as she primed her desire for him was bursting through every pore. I snapped Carol back to the interview. She tried to focus.

'Men, of course, have no idea the amount of time it takes us girls to get ready. They think we are all just natural beauties. In my case, nothing could be further than the truth as it takes time, lots of time, effort, and money!'

In Carol's view, younger men are full of passion, optimism, and ambition for life, not like the jaded blokes her own age. They're often at the start of their careers and full of hopes and dreams, whereas men in their forties and fifties have usually peaked and are on their way down. Her opinion, not mine.

Time had moved on and the man Carol was about to meet was her first date in six months. She was about to meet with a twenty-eight-year-old Spanish surgeon called Juan. 'It was an exciting prospect, but a nerve-racking one,' she recalled.

Having eaten a feast of lobster and desserts that would pile on the pounds, Carol said the date went really well and they clicked in so many ways. She felt so much more confident afterwards, remembering driving home feeling good about herself.

Her next date a week or two later was with another twenty-eight-year-old—an IT specialist named Tom. He had also been found on Tinder. 'It was as if I was fishing with a large net and fish just kept being caught!' She proudly informed me.

Carol met Tom in Oxford, and he'd booked a punt on the river and ordered a Champagne picnic, so Carol thought she would be in for a gorgeously romantic date. But as soon as they had set off, it became obvious that the poor guy had never been in a punt in his life. They spent two hours going around in circles or stuck fast in the river bank. In the end, he had managed to win Carol over just for making her laugh so much.

Carol was on a roll and her next Tinder date a few weeks later was with a twenty-eight-year-old flying instructor named Tim. Not a normal date by any stretch of the imagination, given the date was spent flying over Kent in the UK in a small two-seater aircraft. While Carol recalls the date to have been unique and exhilarating, she didn't have a second date with Tim as, in her words, he was 'not so dashing, carrying too many fat cells and had extremely bad halitosis'.

Carol then made a statement which I found rare; she did not always expect her younger dates to pay but said that doesn't mean she will not take things further than a polite kiss at the end of the night. 'I'm not a cash cow, but I also like to be independent. Some dates seem to think they're meeting some sort of rampant nymphomaniac who's going to drag them off to bed,' she said with a broad smile. 'They're sadly disappointed when I kiss them goodnight and go home alone. Just because I've dated fifteen young men, it doesn't mean I've bedded them all.'

Carol then wanted to tell me about her worst date. It was with a twenty-six-year-old photographer named Chris, who took her to a heavy metal concert in the middle of a muddy field. After an hour of having her stilettos stomped on, her ear drums pierced and beer splashed all over her expensive dress, she made her excuses and fled for the hills. She recalled her expensive shoes were left behind in the mud and she got a lift home barefoot with a truck driver.

The one thing Carol does not do is struggle for conversation. So, any man she dates, I would urge, should be a good listener. Her fashion sense is also out there given it is bold, in your face and not subtle. She commented that one bloke she dated wore his jeans so low on his hips that she kept wanting to pull them up.

'I've been married and widowed and have no interest in doing it again, and the younger men I date aren't at that stage in their lives yet. And, of course, there's also the question of their physical attributes. An upside to dating young men is their beautiful, pert young bodies,' Carol confesses.

'The downside is worrying about my saggy and wrinkly bits. But I've learned that in reality, men don't think that way. It's lovely to be in bed with someone who doesn't have creased skin and doesn't mind being in bed with someone who does. It may sound shallow, but it's true.' Carol sends a half smile.

The youngest man Carol ever dated was Ben, a twenty-two-year-old forensic Mathematics' student. They were together for six months and Carol says she liked him for his intellect as much as his youthful looks. But the age gap did throw up a few embarrassing situations.

'I was mistaken for being his mother by a delivery man.'

'And it was odd when I'd go over to his apartment and find him playing computer games, which made him feel more like a son. Other than that, he was everything I looked for in a man.'

Carol says her friends are accepting of her dating younger men and tend not to judge, but others might not be so tolerant. She has faced the sniggers and whispers from people in bars, clubs, and social occasions. But she adds that she doesn't care what other people think—it is her life. Her married friends specifically, some of whom knew her late husband, are her best supporters.

'Some people will disapprove, which is probably why I don't shout about it at work. But I'm not doing anything wrong.'

'I suspect those who laugh at me might even be a bit jealous. I realize I might get hurt, but that goes for anyone on the dating scene.'

To end this wonderful recount, I asked the man Carol last dated to share his experience. Tony is twenty-eight and works as a style director at a high-class hair salon in London.

In Tony's words, 'I first met Carol two years ago when she tottered into my salon for a makeover. She was, shall I say, a visual impact kind of a woman, given her tight summer dress, sky high-heel shoes, and big red lips. She asked for the best stylist and I, of course, stepped forward. I was instantly drawn to her—she was a buxom with a hot body and an attractive face. The interview proceeded professionally. I say interview because that is how it felt. Carol wanted to know how many years I had been cutting hair, my background, my age, my likes, and dislikes. I could tell she liked me, as the odd flirtatious comment started to come out as we veered off-topic, chatting casually about our weekend plans. On the spur of the moment, I asked her to join me at a club with my friends, but she laughed and said no. I spent the next few hours styling her hair while another colleague tended to her nails and she left looking a million dollars. But before she left the saloon, she asked for my card, on the back of which I had written my phone number.'

'Later that night, after a few drinks, I ended up drunk-dialing her. This was a terrible mistake. I can't remember the exact details, but she humoured me, chatting with me about my night. Surprisingly, she seemed relaxed about the whole thing. More surprisingly, she said she liked me a lot and could see us dating.'

'We continued our causal relationship via text messages, even though we still had not met since her hair appointment. We bonded easily over common interests like music and outdoor activities, and quickly built a tight friendship. Of course, our taste in music was at times divided, but that was alright! We would send flirty text messages to each other throughout the day and late into the night. This lasted for about two weeks before I plucked up the courage to ask her out for drinks again. She agreed and a date was set.'

'Carol selected a fine restaurant and treated me to dinner. It was an evening spent laughing the entire time, and Carol was looking as ravishing as ever in a gold, just-above-the-knee dress. We ended up kissing that night. Despite the age gap, there was definite sexual tension, and I was really attracted to her. Plus, she was fantastic company—outgoing, funny, and spontaneous.'

'After that, we would meet at lunch or after my work at least four times a week. She would pick me up in her car, but always at a distance from the salon. She was very careful because she wanted to protect me from salon gossip. I remember her flipping out when I added her on Facebook, terrified that it would draw attention and I would be laughed at. We eventually progressed to having sex at her Chelsea apartment. It was an apartment that oozed style and taste. Fine works of art, rugs from Persia, and crystal glasses. Sex with Carol was always hot and steamy, and soon I was spending more and more nights over.'

'Despite all the time we spent together, we never had The Talk. Our relationship had no real definition. I knew she was a widow and that it must have been hard for her to start dating again. For a guy, it was the perfect arrangement—she was hot, the sex was great, and there was no commitment. Plus, there were some seriously and unexpected perks. She would buy me expensive tailored shirts, take me away for weekends, and even bought me an expensive Rolex watch.'

'Even though I constantly offered to pay when we went out, she would always pick up the tab, even if we were at a high-end restaurant. She would always send me home after a date even though we lived in opposite ends of the city. She even gave me a smartphone worth over £800 to replace my ratty old model when she picked up a new one for herself. She had no qualms about doing things usually expected of the man in a relationship—paying the bills, driving us around, and constantly having me over at her home.'

'Three months into the relationship, things got even more serious. We would do "couple" things—cancel on our friends to hang out or she'd skip visiting her sister on weekends so we could meet. Yet, at some level, both of us knew the end was near. I was going away to work in a salon overseas, and the age difference meant that we were never going to be a serious item. I think the whole situation worked only on the premise of a definite cut-off point.'

'We eventually decided that things needed to end and met up to awkwardly say our goodbyes. But the night before my flight, Carol asked to see me. When I met her, she passed me an envelope, asking me to open it only when she had left. She told me to have fun in Europe.'

'In the envelope was a huge wad of cash—£1,000, to be exact. I called her up, asking what the money was for. She said she knew she wasn't going to see me again, but just wanted me to be safe in Europe. She told me to keep the money in case of an emergency, as I was going on a shoestring budget. Although I was angry that she'd given me such an unnecessary and extravagant present and I didn't want to feel bought, I was touched by her concern.'

'I never used the money, and I transferred it back to her a few months later when I was promoted and sent back to London. I've never seen her again but we do exchange messages now and then. Looking back, she was an amazing person. Besides being successful and confident, she was also warm, kind, and sincere. It was interesting to be in a relationship where the woman looked after me for a change—a role that's come to be expected of guys. And even though things were mostly physical, there was a real connection.

'My relationship with Carol triggered a change in me. Suddenly, the petty concerns and ridiculous obsessions of women in their early twenties just didn't cut it anymore. Even though I'd had two relationships with girls my age, their insecurities and constant need for reassurance over trivial matters were exhausting compared to the confidence Carol had.'

'Being with an older woman like Carol quickly became something I enjoyed. I knew that the relationships had no emotional foundation or future but that didn't deter me. My cougar magnet days had begun, and Carol had introduced me to a world I would never have considered. She literally opened up my life and I haven't looked back.'

'After Carol, I've been with nine other older women. There was the divorced friend of a friend, two doctors I met in the salon while making them look beautiful, a corporate high-flier—these are just a few. All of them were more than twenty years older than me. I'm not just the typical hair stylist that thinks he is God and I'm a straight male. The salon just presents the perfect place to meet women.'

'My wildest encounter was with two lawyers. I met both of them on a night out and ended up sleeping with both the same night. I didn't even make the first move—they propositioned me twenty minutes after we met. They were both in their fifties. It is not a night I am proud of, but the experience of an older woman is not to be passed up twice.'

'Among all these women, Carol remains the exception—we were a couple in everything but name. With the other women, it was mostly physical. Some were one-night stands, and almost all of the women made the first move.'

At this point I went back to Carol to catch-up and see how she was doing. She, of course, updated me.

'Over the years, though, I've laid out some ground rules. No boyfriend or a husband in the mix, nor a girlfriend on my end.

More importantly, I always make it clear that I'm not seeking a relationship and most of them have been more than happy with this arrangement.'

Interviewing Carol and Tony for this story was fun, insightful, and humorous. I leaned so many things and, in a heartbeat. I would love to have a relationship with a vivacious, proud and sexy woman like Carol. Luckily for her I am older than her, so I wouldn't make the criteria. But it tells us that people make their own decisions, stand by them and enjoy life. Who are w to judge anyone but ourselves. Cougars are just women, women of strong character, intelligence and willpower. I for one am happy such women are around.

PARALLEL UNIVERSE

The Good Seem to Evade the Perfect

I asked myself a question over coffee one morning. The question was this: Why do most single people never meet their perfect soulmate? Let me put this in context. I have written a book *16 SWIPES No Breakfast*, which is about my experiences of dating a number of women who didn't click with me. I then wrote this book about sixteen (plus seven) women who also didn't, in most cases, meet their match or find their soulmate. This then raises another question: What if I had met with these ladies as a single man, would I have been a match for them? It is as if we all seemed to pass by each other in some strange parallel universe. The common thread being that that we were all seeking our soulmates but instead we met those who were simply not right for us. I ask my friends all the time, where are all the nice single women? They simply reply, 'They are everywhere.' Then why is it that I never seem to meet them?

Soulmates—this was not a concept I believed in. It was nothing more than a myth created by someone that watched a lot of romantic movies. That is until by chance I met someone who, for me, ticked every box. I had found my soulmate. While it did not last, and I confess it was my fault, it did prove to me that the myth, in fact, was real. So I started to search for answers to address this question.

It was through a mutual introduction that I met this lady—one who shared an interesting experience with me. No, this was not a romantic connection with any agenda, just someone that had an experience to share. She had just returned from a vacation with her husband in Australia. One morning, as she sipped coffee at the kitchen table in their rented apartment in Queenscliff, Victoria, Australia, looking directly across Swan Bay towards Sorrento, she was fascinated by the passenger ferries that glided across the water every hour or so, shuttling residents and tourists from one town to another.

She had taken the ferry twice herself during their visit. Once, she had hopped off in Sorrento and spent a pleasant afternoon walking along the meandering streets. As she visited cafés, peeked inside the various shops, and listened to the locals, she found herself curious about the history of the town which happened to be the region's first European settlement in Australia. When she returned to Queenscliff later that day, she had a better appreciation for the town she was in and was more aware about the history of both towns.

The second time she had taken that same ferry ride, she had a lengthy but pleasant experience on the boat, while enjoying the sail and observing the dolphins that escorted the ferry into port, going back and forth between the two towns for an entire afternoon. But this time she had decided not to set foot onto the Sorrento shore. Instead, she was preoccupied with enjoying the views and the social scene inside the boat.

This example shows how we make choices in life that are often short-sighted. Given the opportunity for a 'do-over', she made time for a richer experience in Sorrento each time she had the opportunity. She really had no idea when, or if, she would ever get back there.

All too often, the second type of ferry experience happens in relationships. Each partner moves in a hurried, independent fashion through daily life, preoccupied with his or her own desires. Sometimes one partner will wave to the other from afar, but neither takes the time to discover who the other truly is and revel in the special, deep joy each can bring to the relationship.

In short, by being like 'two ships that pass in the night', the opportunity to meet someone new and experience a state of togetherness in the relationship is missed. Many relationships have foundered, like a sinking ship, and ultimately ended, mostly due to each partner's preoccupation with their own career or surroundings.

This in part did address my question, in that perhaps we all need to explore more why some relationships or connections don't last. Do we actually learn from failures? As for me, how could I fully set my mind at ease and also help women out there also learn from this? If not, the natural course, if untended, is to drift apart and become the proverbial two ships passing in the night.

When I was at university, occasionally I'd hear a professor say, 'I really enjoy teaching. It's the students I can't stand.' In contrast, when I worked in consulting, occasionally I'd hear a fellow consultant say, 'Selling wouldn't be so bad if it weren't for the customers.'

What I and they didn't understand was 'relationship'—the importance of a relationship and the process of relationship. The same thing can be said about any marriage or relationship or a team relationship. There are five things to know and to action to make it all work.

1. *Get a realistic understanding of what a relationship is and what it is not. If you find the definitive answer to this, write a book on it.*

    As marriage therapists have recorded, 'Marriage is, in fact, just a way of living. Before marriage, we don't expect life to be all sunshine and roses, but we seem to expect marriage to be that way. Why is this so? I believe that by dispelling the myth of eternal romance will do more than just about anything to help build a lifelong, happy marriage?

    I'm reminded of the lawyer who handled my divorce case and told me that the No. 1 reason two people split up is that they 'refuse to accept the fact that they are married to a human being'. The belief in a happily-ever-after marriage is one of the most widely held and destructive marriage myths prevalent today. This is also true when searching for the perfect person to date—dispel the expectation that the first date will go as you intend.

    Likewise, corporate teams would be better off to get a realistic understanding of a team relationship. Teams are just another way of working. And there *will* be problems . . . that *will* require some patience and skill to get to the outcomes you want.

2. *Get a realistic perception of the other person.*

    The most dramatic loss experienced in a new marriage or relationship is the idealized image the two partners have of one another. Sooner or later, reality will hit the two people squarely in the face—they did not marry or enter a relationship with the person they *thought* they did.

    That's why author John Fisher advises, 'The success of a marriage and relationships comes not in finding the "right" person, but in the ability of both partners to adjust to the real person they inevitably realize they are now with.'

3. *Engage in meaningful communication.*
   According to Gary Smalley, the author of several books on marital communication, 'Many couples, in thinking they know each other intimately, have actually lived on a superficial level for years. Unfortunately, marriages of this type are the norm rather than the exception.'

   In essence, they have failed to communicate. Oh, they may talk, but that's quite different from real communication. Talking is sharing facts, such as 'I'll be home late from work or let's have a Chinese for dinner.'

   Communication is spending quality time together . . . sharing who you really are, what you think, and how you feel. And many adults are afraid of sharing their feelings . . . or are 'too busy' for any in-depth communication with their spouse or partner. As a result, these people find themselves five years into a relationship or ten years into a marriage and still very lonely. They discover that their loneliness has nothing to do with their proximity to the other person. It comes from a lack of deeper, ongoing communication.

   It is important to remind ourselves of the natural course of things that if untended, it is easy to drift apart and become the proverbial two ships that pass in the night.

   So, what is the solution to this? If you are in a relationship or are married, you both have to ask the brave questions. Learn about each other and understand that talking is not communicating unless you are exploring each other and their reactions to certain situations.

4. *Stay focused on your goal.*

    It's what distinguishes two people who are 'merely' living together or dating and two people who are 'truly' married. Truly married people have a common goal they are pursuing.

    It's what distinguishes each of us and when this goal aligns with your partner, you have a strong match.

    This became clear to me one evening when listening to a keynote speaker at a charity evening. The speaker talked about climbing Mt Everest—the skills it took, the dangers that had to be handled, the people who made it to the top, and those who didn't.

    But just before he finished his speech, he asked the audience a question. 'There's a time when you're climbing when you almost feel depressed. You feel so low and down you're not sure you can continue. Do you know when that is?'

    The audience shouted out their answers. No one was came close to the truth.

    The speaker said, 'Climbers get down when bad weather sets in.' And, then went on to explain that when bad weather sets in you can't see the peak. You lose sight of your *goal* and become easily distracted and sometimes even depressed.

    Of course, you might be wondering what this has to do with answering my question—why do good people pass by each other without ever really meeting?

    There's a very clear correlation. Like a mountain climber who can't see the peak, single people who can't see their clearly defined goals are more susceptible to distractions and more likely to waste their time on the less important things in life. Meaning you think you are searching, but how much efforts are you really putting in?

So, ask yourself if your search for a perfect partner has a clearly defined goal. If not, get one. Get a goal and keep your eye on the goal.

5. *Respect differences.*

In the initial stages of a relationship, differences tend to attract. We find them fascinating. But often times, those same differences can become a source of irritation later on in the relationship.

That's too bad, because differences are the source of power, but when they're acknowledged, respected, and utilized.

So, learn to celebrate differences and use each other's strengths. Don't waste your time trying to pound the differences out of the other person or make the other person just like you. It's self-defeating, and it won't work anyway.

For starters, you will always find exceptions to the rule, but research and experience consistently point to a fundamental and powerful distinction between the sexes: Men focus on achievement; women focus on relationships. It sounds overly simplistic, and it probably is. But remembering this general rule can save every couple wear and tear and strengthen their bond.

So, I have now found my answer: it's either that fate has played a hand or there is a parallel universe, or simply and more believable, we are not setting the right goal, communicating well enough, or we simply facing pure old bad luck.

WOMEN

The World Will Become Female

In this book, I wanted to somehow honour and celebrate women. Female diversity and inclusion is a subject that finds its way into mass media these days as we see and hear about women that are considered role models not just for diversity, but for all of us in that they head multi-billion dollar organizations or inspire us as entrepreneurs. We are all equal, and we are all important and we all matter. The women featured in this book have helped me better appreciate the struggles they face. It has made me both laugh and cry and also feel ashamed. In summary, this book has set out what I had hoped it would achieve. It presents the female perspective; all seen through a lens of online dating experiences.

So, this chapter takes all of the confessions and attempts at finding the love and the hurt these women faced and presents my view on how I see the world shaping in the future. Perhaps then, and only then, will some men give them the respect they deserve.

It is time for the women of the world to reject inferior status, demand equality, and unapologetically go forth and revel in their ambition and success. We celebrate International

Women's Day every year, and why not, I say. I'm proud to support such initiatives, and I have had in my life many female role models, from my own mother to female bosses, celebrities and politicians.

I read an article once that touched my heart. Many years ago, during a time of racial tension in the US, a mother handed her daughter a piece of folded-up paper with a message she thought she would need. She had written in longhand on a page torn from a little notebook she had kept by the phone.

It read: 'No one can make you feel inferior without your consent.'

It's a quote widely attributed to Eleanor Roosevelt, and it was a wonderful gift for a young woman setting off into the world.

It's worth reflecting on the words in that note for a second. The key word is 'feel'. You see, the little girl that was handed that note was an African American. Her mother was acutely aware that a person, and a woman, in particular, could be shoved into a lower rank in a very real and profound way. Laws could dictate where people could live or work and whether one could own a property or even vote. Customs and social mores and self-appointed status checkers could keep one out of the boardroom or the clubhouse. But no one actually has the power to reach inside the soul of another and turn down the dial of their self-confidence. The mother who had handwritten that note had a strong work ethic, but she also has a fierce 'worth ethic'. Self-regard in the face of oppression was her superpower.

That word—power—takes on different dimensions when viewed through a gendered lens. Power is most often associated with strength, which in turn is linked to physical prowess or financial might. The default assumption is that all of society benefits when men are raised to become powerful—their families, their communities, their places of work, and even worship if you have a religious faith. When women talk about exerting power or flexing their collective might by coming together, the assumptions are very different. It's too often seen as a zero-sum game, in which women gain power at the expense of men and the peril of society.

Could we finally be at a turning point in society? I came of age during the 1970s, a period of protests, political changes, great music, and bad fashion trends. But above all, it was a time that seemed to be very macho. Women have been marching and picketing and demanding their rights way before I was even born. And as with most movements, progress comes in fits and starts, times of setbacks and periods that feel like a flash of momentum. The Equal Rights Amendment first drafted in 1923, seemed certain to be ratified by the early 1970s but it stalled. We are now in another moment of sweeping progress, most evident in the #MeToo movement that gained global attention following misconduct by a former Hollywood movie mogul and an astounding upwelling of emboldened and infuriated women saying time's up to sexual harassment and assault. That revolt has produced a new wave of legislation, greater awareness, and immediate consequences for men who had previously got away with a pass or slap on the wrist for predatory behaviour. A former Hollywood movie mogul certainly had his day in court. Veterans in the struggle for women's rights, used to disappointment, are hoping this really is a long-lasting movement, not just another flash in time.

This is an era of outrage and division, but we are seeing strong reasons for optimism. We are all witnessing an age when women step-up. We live in a time, ladies and gentlemen, when a woman can become a four-star general or an Oscar-winning film director or a Fortune 500 CEO, and one even became the speaker of the House of Representatives in the US.

Around the globe, women are gaining unprecedented power. Nearly two-thirds of the Spanish government's cabinet ministers are women. The only country that banned women from driving, Saudi Arabia, has finally allowed it. Women have led almost a third of the world's countries.

In a seismic development, the US women's national soccer team dominated the World Cup with such force, consistency, and chutzpah that it outperformed the US men's team in victories, viewership, and pop culture status. When you mention American soccer today, women are the ones who symbolize the sport. Yet, we still live at a time when these megastars are fighting in court to ensure they are paid the same as men. In fact, it's not even about equal pay for equal work; it's equal pay for demonstrably more successful work. These are women who strut their success, revel in their triumphs on the field, and become role models for women seeking to challenge the basis for their second-class status.

For centuries women have been viewed as the weaker, more vulnerable gender. They have been rendered inferior, not necessarily with their consent, but with considerable help from social constructs and scientific research. Not anymore, things are changing.

So, let's ask ourselves, why do men hold more power than women today? Why does gender inequality persist? The explanation is so often this: *It's just the way it's always been.* But that's simply not good enough anymore. And that justification should crumble in the face of evidence showing that places with policies hampering or oppressing women lose ground economically. Take Asia as an example. A region I know well, as I live in Asia. Slightly more than half of the region's women work, and those women are paid less than men. Gender norms, barriers to education, and entrenched cultural forces could maintain that status quo, but analysts warn that countries impeding the advancement of women will pay a steep price. The consulting firm McKinsey & Company estimates that the regional economy would gain as much as $4.5 trillion in annual GDP by 2025, if women are no longer side-lined in the Asian workforce. That is a staggering statistic to digest. In my humble opinion, every country should take notice. Those t-shirts and posters that read 'The future is female' should warn instead 'The future had better be female!'

But before we all break out the bubbly—and some of us may consider rushing off to Bangkok for a sex change, which of course is fine—the obstacles to power are deeply ingrained and aren't so easily changed or overcome. You can write laws telling people what they can and cannot do, but you cannot legislate their feelings about themselves or others. If only that were possible. We are still ambivalent about women and power. Studies suggest that women are more apt to be deemed 'unlikeable' or 'untrustworthy' if they are perceived to be powerful, brash, or openly ambitious. These are traits that, by the way, are seen as management material in men. Sadly, as a society, we are demonstrating a degree of trepidation and surprise about women taking the reins of power, because it's still a novel concept. Women who become speakers of the house, Facebook CFOs, Bankers, and billionaire entrepreneurs are not just hailed as mavericks. They are also practically portrayed as unicorns. The greatest barrier that many women have to overcome is experience. Again, studies find that men are often hired for 'potential', while women with the same experience are deemed underqualified.

Our collective cultural narrative contributes to this bias. The phrase 'women's work' is limiting and stereotypical by being attached to softer domestic tasks thought to be the work of women. Cooking. Cleaning. Tending to children. But the fact is, women have been holding up half the world while toiling in jobs considered 'men's work'. I once wrote a screenplay titled *The Canary Girls* inspired by my grandmother who toiled in the British munition factories during World War II, while the men were off fighting. She worked longer hours, lifted the same weight, and suffered great illnesses as a result. It is so important for women to see what they can do and become, so it is not just in their imaginations.

In closing, remember that quote attributed to Eleanor Roosevelt? She may not have even said it, but hey, many think she did, and it does not really matter. The fact is someone wrote those words and they mean something. People invested in the status quo will always be looking for people who can be made to feel inferior. It's the glass floor they stand on. But in this moment, where there's so much promise and so much at stake, let's make sure that it's no longer easy to find women who can be made to feel inferior. Let's make sure they know their power and their place—as equals. So, men of the world, take note.

MY OWN REFLECTION

To Sum It All Up

A couple of months ago, I was sitting at a bar, sipping a Gin and Tonic, a Four Pillars distil in case you were wondering, minding my own business when the woman next to me did something to catch my attention. It was a strange act given she was surrounded by potential partners—all single men. She pulled out her phone and opened the online dating app Tinder. On her screen, images of men appeared and then disappeared in rapid flow to the left and right, depending on the direction in which she swiped her finger.

I felt a sense a rejection—not personally—but on behalf of all the single men at the bar, and clearly on the hunt. Instead of interacting with the men around her, she chose to search for a companion online. It confirmed to me that online dating has impacted how we interact. It's creating a new reality in which people actively avoid real-life interactions. Of course, others have raised these sorts of questions before. But the fear that online dating is changing us collectively, that it's creating unhealthy habits and preferences that aren't in our best interests, is being driven more by paranoia than it is by actual facts.

One of the first things you have to know to understand how dating—or really courtship rituals, since not everyone calls it dating—has changed over time is that the age of marriage in the US and the UK has increased dramatically. In the past, people used to marry in their early twenties, which meant that most dating or courting was done with the intention of settling down right away. But that's not the life that young people lead anymore. The age of first marriage is now in the late twenties, and more people in their thirties and even forties are deciding not to settle down. The rise of phone apps and online dating websites give people access to more potential partners than they can meet at work or in the communities within which they live. It makes it easier for someone who is looking for something very specific in a partner to find what they are looking for. It also helps the people who use the apps by allowing them to enjoy a pattern of regular hook-ups that don't have to lead to relationships. I think these things are characteristics of modern romance.

Given this observation, I decided to interview a number of people to understand their experiences. This is what I deduced: As many as 1 in 10 people in the age group of 20–60 years use one or another online dating platform. Because this social phenomenon is relatively new, little research has been conducted to examine the impact that online dating has on culture. People's expectations and realities of online dating and the mobile applications used to access them, whether they deem their experiences as positive or negative, are indeed varied. These experiences also include deception and discrimination by others, which is surprising given so many people now turn to these platforms in search of love, romance, fun or friendship, and represent all cultures and races. For many reasons, many believe they are discriminated against based on their physical appearance; others believe they have been lied to, but few perceive themselves as lying; and overall, most perceive online dating as positive and a normal thing to do. Humans have an ingrained primal need to feel purpose and inclusion. Young adults between 18 and 25 years are particularly driven to belong, and often use their relationships with others as a way to shape their own identity. Even adults, ages 45–60, now turn to this form of meeting people to find love. One way that people achieve this is through the acquisition of meaningful romantic partnerships. In this day and age, more and more young people are turning to online dating sites and mobile phone applications in search of love and intimacy. From the launch of the first online dating site in 1995 to the invention of modern social networking dating sites in 2007, online dating has grown into a multi-billion-dollar industry with countless users. In fact, today nearly four billion people worldwide use some form of online dating.

Tinder, described in more detail later, is just one of many mobile dating applications designed for use on mobile phones and boasts millions of users—63 per cent of which are young adults aged 18–24. As many as 66 per cent of these users go on to date individuals they meet online and 23 per cent form long-term relationships with individuals they meet on these sites. Utilization rates of online dating sites are relatively equal between men and women.

As a growing number of individuals participate in online dating, issues unique to this method of finding partnerships have developed. One such issue of interest is how online dating and mobile applications are changing and affecting the dating culture of the people who use them and how people perceive these experiences. It is possible that the popularity of dating applications is not only encouraging young and old adults to 'date shop', but also select potential mates based on limited visual data versus connecting via conversation. Furthermore, forming relationships based on such limited information can also encourage users to make judgments about others based on biases. These factors have the potential to have long-term effects on how individuals form attachments.

There are now countless research papers on this topic. This research specifically explores people's expectations of online dating and mobile applications, their realities, whether they deem their experiences as positive or negative with the attempt to gauge the extent that their relational styles are shaped by using these applications.

If we look at the realities of usage—when asked what they actually did with the people they met on these sites—the people I surveyed indicated going on dates as the most common response. Some of the people I asked indicated that they developed short-term casual romantic relationships, some just hooked up for sex, and some reported doing nothing. Meeting new people and developing long-term relationships were fewer common responses. Lastly, a few people I spoke with indicated having done 'other' things with the people they met online. One can only wonder what that was. But, when asked to specify what those things were, they wrote: 'Nothing, just had some adult fun. And there was more than one person involved.' I think we can leave the rest to imagination.

That said. These findings do suggest that, of this sample, a sizable number of adults use online dating sites, particularly apps like Tinder for a variety of reasons. Of these, curiosity and the potential for dating were the most common reasons stated by many. This is reflected by the fact that most people actually went on dates or developed relationships with people they met online. So, something positive did come out of it. But we are not done yet. What about how these people presented themselves, to what extent did users represent themselves honestly? So, I asked whether people felt like their matches had been intentionally dishonest on these sites; what they believed their matches were dishonest about; and if they themselves had ever been intentionally dishonest; and if so, what they were dishonest about.

About 30 per cent of the people I talked to, indicated that they believed they had been lied to or were unsure, and a large number, about 60 per cent said they had not been honest about who they were and what they were looking for in a relationship. The main areas of their dishonesty were regarding their appearance, their interests, and their age. Less common were weight or height. Despite feeling that they had been intentionally lied to by others, the majority of the participants indicated that they themselves had not been intentionally dishonest to potential matches online. In summary, most believed they had been deceived but denied intentionally deceiving themselves. These findings suggest that there is a disconnect between the percentage of people who thought they were deceived compared to the percentage that admitted to being dishonest.

In conclusion, the internet has transformed the way people work and communicate. Tell me something I don't know—I hear you say. But think about it for a moment. It has upended industries, from entertainment and fashion to retailing. But its most profound effect may well be on the biggest life decision that most people make—choosing a partner.

In the early 1990s, the notion of meeting a partner online seemed freakish, if not a little pathetic. Today, it is considered very normal. In fact, more people would think you were weird if you had not tried an online dating site. Smartphones have put virtual bars, nightclubs, cafes, and meeting places in people's pockets where singletons can mingle free from the constraints of social or physical geography. Globally, at least 400 million people use digital dating services every month. In America, more than a third of marriages now start with an online match-up. The internet is now the most popular way for people to meet people of the opposite sex and has replaced the 'friend of a friend' introductions and pot luck chances you have, should you visit a social scene like a bar, club or café. So, in today's world, online dating is a popular component of youth and adult culture that continues to grow. Where it will stop, nobody knows. Perhaps one day in the not too distant future, we will see virtual partners emerge, as we have seen depicted in sci-fi movies. We will perhaps even be able to design our own partner of choice, select anything from body type, hair colour, age, skin colour, voice tone, and language, and even behaviour. We can pre-programme our partners to be submissive or dominant, switch them on and off at will. Perhaps when that day comes, it will be the end of real human interaction.

A WOMAN'S INSIGHT

What Women Want

'I'll come right out and say it: I *love* online dating', replied Jo, the woman I was interviewing while chilling out over coffee.

She went on to explain. Having experienced more than a fair share of dating, she could say with confidence that there was no other medium out there that allowed a girl to get twenty-eight dates—most of them with different men—in thirty days. Between her memberships on Tinder, Match.com, and Coffee Meets Bagel, she found it easy to find interesting men who wanted to take her out on a date. She informed me that she could go on all day about how women should spruce up their profiles to meet interesting men, but instead, she shared the secrets of what she—and I suspect most women—look for in a man's dating profile. This is what I learned from her.

1. *First impressions count.*
   An eye-catching first impression—compare the contents and information of an online dating profile to that of a professional resume and cover letter that one would send as part of a job application. This information is your chance

to attract attention and showcase everything that makes you completely 'dateable'. If you fail to create a profile that adequately reflects your qualities and strengths as a potential 'candidate', you run the chances of being overlooked. Also remember, when women join a dating site, they are most often looking for a lasting relationship.

One of the many benefits of online dating is that it takes a lot of the guesswork out of the dating scene by asking other members to list their interests, qualities, hobbies, and aspirations out in the open. Use this as an opportunity to really showcase yourself. This, she said, would trigger a woman wanting to know more about you.

2. *Be creative, be unique.*
Jo continued. Be original, creating the profile for your respective online dating site is an opportunity to provide women users with a snippet of your personality. I repeat, Be original! Avoid clichés like 'I like to live life to the fullest' and 'I enjoy romantic walks on the beach'. Those phrases are boring and more importantly, overdone. They do not provide any real information about who you are. Try to examine your life values and interests and put those things into words. Stand out from the crowd and be creative. Use a description of yourself that is unique and exciting. That is much more likely to catch a woman's eye. You have some very exceptional interests and qualities that are going to be very attractive to another person. It's time to expose them.

Of course, you can't tell someone everything about yourself through an online profile. However, you can get creative and attract attention. Incorporate things that are going to make you stand out. If you could choose one superpower, what would it be? Things like this are going to be remembered, and the purpose of your online profile is going to serve as an audition for the real show—the first date.

3. *Don't be afraid to show your soft side.*
   Show your sensitive side guys. Women know that you spend a lot of your free time playing sport, watching sports and 'broing out' with your mates in a bar while throwing back beers. Jo points out here not to misunderstand her point. 'Don't get me wrong; having the ability to be a man's man is an attractive feature in a partner', she says. However, women also like to experience your softer, intellectual side. Look at this as an opportunity to let your sensitive and cultured qualities shine through. You may not get a chance to talk about your love for classic novels, describe your adorable cuddle sessions with your Labrador retriever or confess to crying when you watched *The Notebook*. These may not be appropriate topics for a poker night, but we certainly want to hear about them. We want a burly, manly man with a soft spot. Give us a preview of both angles.

4. *Stay humble and down-to-earth.*
   Be confident, just not too confident. Confidence can be a very attractive quality in a man. Women want a man that is aware of what he has to offer, knows how to use it and most importantly, in choosing her as the recipient of this gift. However, use discretion and be careful not to create a profile that could potentially come across as vain or egotistical. Be aware of your tone in your written descriptions. State your strengths with confidence but don't be arrogant. If you are

an active individual and have the physique to prove it, we want to see that. Instead of posting a selfie of you flexing in the mirror, use a photo from a day at the lake with friends. Your abs will most certainly not go unnoticed and we will take note of your choice of pictures, seeing that your friends are important to you.

5. *Show them what sets you apart from the rest.*
   What do you have to offer? Very often, online dating site users view their profiles as a chance to display what they are looking for in a partner instead of exhibiting what they have to offer. It's certainly okay to give some indication of what qualities you are looking for, as well. However, your efforts are better served to describe yourself as a person and potential companion and letting women know what treatment to expect from you.

   You have something to offer women that others don't. It's time to figure out what that is and own it. Maybe you give shoulder massages second to none. Maybe you have an unusually high tolerance for chick flicks, are the perfect shopping companion or are a phenomenal listener. What makes you great? Find out what these qualities are and make sure to let women know. Not only will you be advertising your strengths as a potential boyfriend, but you will also gain confidence from knowing all of the things that make you desirable.

6. *Authenticity goes a long way.*
   Be yourself. Be confident about who you are and what you have to offer. Tell the truth. One of the most sought-after benefits of online dating is that profiles are used to

put important information out there. Female users that may come across your profile may notice a 'deal-breaking' detail right away, saving you both time and embarrassment by catching it upfront instead of on the first or second date. It is equally as likely that they will notice a quality that is exactly on par with what they are seeking. You want someone to give you a shot because they like what they saw. More importantly, you want the things they saw to be the real you.

Choose the perfect pictures to show who you are and what you are about. Be selective and deliberate when deciding which photos to include. This is not only a chance for women to see what you look like, but it also allows them another glimpse into your persona. Include action shots of you doing something fun and exciting to show your adventurous side.

'If you have an exciting life, show us.' Jo shares. Consider a photo of you hiking, mountain biking or fishing. Including a picture with family and friends illustrates the importance of the relationships in your life. One word—puppies. Posting a photo of you with an animal of any kind is likely to melt the heart of any woman who stumbles upon your profile. Include photos that you may have taken on a trip to Europe or a cruise to the Caribbean. This is the perfect chance to provide a visual representation of how diverse and exciting your interests are. When creating your profile for an online dating site it is important to be strategic and purposeful with the information you share. Knowing what women are looking for as they browse different profiles will help you determine a plan of action. Consider these tips when deciding on which of your qualities and personality details to include in your profile. I'm here to provide you with a little bit of insight into what women are thinking as they search for the love of their life from behind their computer screens. So, guys, you now know what women want to see should you have a profile on a dating site.

EPILOGUE

Looking Back

Having looked back at the experiences these ladies endured, those that are still active on Tinder have shared that they are now finding a lot more enjoyment swiping through profiles and reading what people have to say about themselves than actually finding Mr Right. Tinder has almost become an addiction.

It's interesting to observe a generation that dictates that everyone is unique, that everyone is an individual. Despite us cynically rolling our eyes at people who conform or follow trends, they have deduced that many of the profiles they view carry the same bland descriptions, cynical quirks, one-liners, and even style of photos. Consider these trite examples:

- The dude holding up a fish.
- The professional self-declared Netflix binger.
- Not a picture of you, just of your dog or cat.
- I won't show my face but I will show you the picture of a tropical beach or a plate of food.
- The classic 'I love long walks on the beach.'

- I like to go on adventures.
- I'm a military veteran, but really I'm a Nigerian scammer.

So, I'm sure others too have their own personal favourites of the dating app constants and clichés, but here are some ways to make your profile stand out and a tiny bit more of a 'swipe right' contender.

There are endless questions that can spin in our heads before, during, and after a date, which is why I have compiled a list of some top dating tips for men and women, to help make sure your date is an ultimate success.

1. *First impressions are always important.* Your ripped jeans may be lucky, but remember, this will be the first impression your date gets of you. Yes, you should never pretend to be someone that you're not, but a girl or a guy might like to see that you take pride in your appearance. Don't worry, this doesn't mean you need to wear a full tuxedo or ball gown, but having a shower, a shave, wax your legs, and putting on something suitable will help you impress your date and get you off to a good start. Now all you have to worry about is turning up on time.
2. *Make date plans for somewhere you'll both feel comfortable.* Dating can be a daunting experience. If she or he has asked you to pick somewhere, help cut through those nerves by arranging to meet up in familiar territory. This will help make you both feel more comfortable. Although, maybe avoid your normal Saturday night pub or club, as bumping into your mates could be a little distracting on your date.
3. *Be confident.* Across the board, confidence is attractive and enthusiasm will make you shine. If you're a little shy,

practice beforehand by talking to people you don't know. Or, while on the date, pick a subject that you're enthusiastic about, such as a hobby. She or he will sense your confidence as you talk passionately about it. Many people may also be shy about their appearance. You may not be six-feet tall with a six-pack, or six-feet tall with legs that go on forever, but it's more attractive to a woman or man to show that you're comfortable in your own skin and happy being you.

4. *Don't do all the talking.* On your date, make sure you don't do all the talking. If this date goes well, there will be lots more opportunities to share your stories in the future. Don't be scared of pauses and help mix up the conversation by asking your date questions. Listening is important, as it shows that you are interested in what she has to say.

5. *Keep the conversation fun.* Light-hearted is the key. On your first date, you don't want to get into an in-depth conversation about why you don't enjoy your job, or other issues you've been having like a former husband, wife of boyfriend. Yes, you do have to be serious sometimes, but in the early stages of dating, have some fun.

6. *Avoid the 'ex' conversation.* Talking about your ex is dangerous territory. It's best to stay away from the conversation altogether. It's unlikely that your date will be interested, and it can make things feel awkward between you. If your date does bring up the subject, try to keep answers short, without appearing suspicious. Reassure him or her that your past is history and that you want to spend your time getting to know her instead.

7. *Turn off your phone.* There's nothing more annoying than phones ringing or beeping whilst trying to spend quality time out with friends, and it's just as irritating on a date.

Don't just put it on silent or vibrate, as it can still be distracting. Turn your phone off completely. If he or she knows that you've turned your phone off to focus entirely on the date, they will appreciate you're taking the time to engage fully.

8. *Share the bill.* Whether you're a dating feminist or an alpha-male, most men and women will assume that they are paying for their share of the bill. It may be worth letting your date know towards the beginning of your date, just so you're both on the same page. In the early stages of dating, you want your date to be spending time with you because they like you, rather than because they think they owe you something.

9. *Follow up correctly after your date.* If you don't want a second date, don't say you'll call them and never do. You'll end up feeling bad and they might feel hurt. Just say, 'I had a great time tonight.' If you do want to see them again, don't play games. Yes, in films they always leave it a couple of days to contact each other, but this is real life. If you don't contact them within a couple of days, you'll seem like you couldn't be bothered, or didn't enjoy the date. The sooner you tell them what a great time you had, the better.

10. *Get feedback from a friend.* Dating is not something we learn at school; we simply have to jump in the deep end and see how it goes. But, if you're looking to improve your dating skills, why not talk to a friend? Discuss your last date, where you went, what you did and what you talked about. Everyone has different opinions, but it can help to give you some useful feedback on how to be better on your next date.

11. *Post pictures that are clear, nicely angled, and show your face.* Nice, clean selfies are an absolute must. I can't tell you

how many times I have seen profiles of folks shadowed in a sunset, or hidden behind a massive pair of sunglasses, or of their backs. Let me see you! Show photos of yourself, else... what is the point? Would you buy something without seeing it first? Your photos are a reflection of you. Mirror selfies of your abs aren't necessary. It ain't the classiest thing to have a mirror selfie (especially with flash) showing off your body. You might have a great one, but you don't really want to come off as being only proud of your body and nothing else. There are a lot of better ways to show off your figure and a cute outfit can show off your definition in a very attractive way. I'm not telling you to censor or discredit anything of the sort, but you may give the wrong first impression.

12. *Don't expect people to search for you in a crowd.* Your dress/suit must have been 'da bomb' during your formal or on this particular outing with your friends, but some can't be bothered to flip through group pictures and pick you out from a crowd. It's great to know you're sociable and have friends, but I want to date *you* and not your social group.

13. *Make your description memorable.* Here's a fun example you might want to consider: 'If you look at my profile, I'm a total dweeb but both lines have a rhyme to it.' I try to keep things succinct and fun to read, while explaining a little bit about myself and what I'm looking for. From this, people can infer that I game, like horror movies, or that I love to colour my hair. They grasp my gender and know I'm looking for someone witty, good-looking, and nerdy. I'm making it clear the sort of person that I am in my brief two lines.

14. *Don't just list your majors.* Everybody likes food and Netflix. You don't have to write an essay but let them know a

little about what makes you special. We've been writing about ourselves since school. I'm sure you can muster up something that would make others laugh or want to know more.

15. *Smile.* Don't be shy! Show off those pearly whites. I get how some people want to look different but that can only get you so far. I promise that if we meet in person, I don't want you to be a stick in the mud. Smiles are contagious, and good ones are often a reason to swipe right.

16. *Do not fear judgment.* I don't care if some people think that Tinder or Bumble is dumb. The fact is nobody cares. You signed up, you wrote your profile, you added pictures, and you're actively swiping. You're a part of this just like anyone of us, and you declaring your cynical disdain for this particular app melts you into the negative crowd. Either be positive or get off the app.

Although some of these points may seem like I'm stating the obvious, but I spent a chunk of time swiping and reading profiles. Dating should be fun, and you should be proud to put yourself out there and explore the world of romance with the rest of us. We're all on these sorts of apps for different reasons, but clarity, transparency, and honesty are all good things to show off for yourself.

What you need to know about dating a fifty-year-old man

When you join a dating website or meet a prospective partner in real life, remember that age has become more and more irrelevant today. Seniors are living longer and enjoying a better quality of life than in past generations. Age really has become just a number. As the average life expectancy goes up, a man who is fifty in 2020 can on an average, look forward to another thirty years of life to enjoy.

Age can be largely defined by someone's perspective and attitude, and today fifty really can be the new forty! You have so many opportunities to meet singles and try different experiences, so what do you need to know when dating a fifty-year-old man?

I have dated fifty-year-old women. Given I am fifty-six, there is nothing out of the ordinary about this. Prior to these encounters, I spent a significant amount of time dating women both in this age group and younger, much younger. I have found that a woman of this age also exhibits some characteristics of Generation X and has many individual qualities worthy of attention. Looking back, I've learned that a fifty-year-old woman is tuned in to different things than she was in her younger days. The same can be said for men.

Men in their twenties, thirties, and forties are still proving themselves. Many are raising kids. Some men are middle-aged, part of Generation X, and may have had a mid-life crisis, and now likes enjoying things that he missed while being tied down. He makes more time for his interests, but he's still capable of making time together.

There are decades to worry about such things. He should have his finances in order, a home that is almost paid for, and has time for exploring the dating world. His career, although it could be at its peak, doesn't demand as much attention as when he was starting out.

He has had at least one long-term relationship. He might have close ties to his children and, possibly, to young grandchildren. These connections are important, but he believes his children are responsible for their own lives.

He may have fifteen to twenty years left to work, but how much he earns and saves now will greatly impact his golden years. He may not pursue a relationship that requires changing employment or location if this is the case. He is financially wise and will splurge on special occasions and budget for his favourite things.

Physically, he can still do many activities and have intimate adventures, but he tires more easily. Some men in this age group seek medical assistance for their sex lives, but they are still interested and active. Be supportive and remind him, that you're there to date the whole person he is. There are still many ways to enjoy a healthy sex life at this age.

We're all creatures of habit, but we have more flexibility in our younger years. The fifty-year-old man can be attached to his routines, including meal times, how he spends days off, and grooming rituals. He may not go out on a weeknight if it will conflict with his bedtime or stay out too late on the weekend. But he may also embrace hobbies he hasn't tried in decades, such as riding a motorcycle.

If this man came out of a long marriage, he might have enjoyed the stability and may still be friends with his former partner. Now he needs to find himself as a lover. He may not want to remarry, but he could feel comfortable in a serious relationship. Although he might take his time to commit, getting to know him will help you understand his relationship goals.

With age, comes wisdom. There are many things he has achieved or tried once but now he is settled in who he is, and he seeks substance. He may want to date someone with the same interests, but he's really seeking someone who exhibits the key attributes he values and that are compatible with his life.

Dating middle-aged men presents different challenges for men and women. A man of fifty feels responsible for kids, grandkids, and aging parents. It's can be hard to be in the sandwich generation because it's exhausting to help everyone. Let a mature man show you the characteristics that matter most to him. He may not be initially very open with his affections, but he could be your ideal match.

If you are you single and looking for love? Are you finding it hard to meet the right person? When you're having trouble finding a love connection, it's all too easy to become discouraged or buy into the destructive myths out there about dating and relationships.

Life as a single person offers many rewards, such as being free to pursue your own hobbies and interests, learning how to enjoy your own company, and appreciating the quiet moments of solitude. However, if you're ready to share your life with someone and want to build a lasting, worthwhile relationship, life as a single person can also seem frustrating.

For many of us, our emotional baggage can make finding the right romantic partner a difficult journey. Perhaps, you grew up in a household where there was no role model of a solid, healthy relationship, and you doubt that such a thing even exists. Or, maybe your dating history consists only of brief flings and you don't know how to make a relationship last. You could be attracted to the wrong type of person or keep making the same bad choices over and over, due to an unresolved issue from your past. Or maybe you're not putting yourself in the best environments to meet the right person, or that when you do, you don't feel confident enough.

Whatever the case may be, you can overcome your obstacles. Even if you've been burned repeatedly or have a poor track record when it comes to dating, these tips can help put you on the path to finding a healthy, loving relationship that lasts.

Above all remember these pointers, a healthy relationship is when two people develop a connection based on:

- Mutual respect
- Trust
- Honesty
- Support
- Fairness/equality
- Separate identities
- Good communication
- A sense of playfulness/fondness

Distinguish between what you want and what you need in a partner. Wants are negotiable, needs are not. Wants include things like occupation, intellect, and physical attributes such as height, weight, and hair colour. Even if certain traits seem crucially important at first, over time you'll often find that you've been needlessly limiting your choices. For example, it may be more important to find someone who is:

- Curious rather than extremely intelligent. Curious people tend to grow smarter over time, while those who are bright may languish intellectually if they lack curiosity
- Sensual rather than sexy
- Caring rather than beautiful or handsome
- A little mysterious rather than glamorous
- Humorous rather than wealthy

- From a family with similar values to yours, rather than someone from a specific ethnic or social background

Needs are different than wants in that needs are those qualities that matter to you most, such as values, ambitions, or goals in life. These are probably not the things you can find out about a person by eyeing them on the street, reading their profile on a dating site, or sharing a quick cocktail at a bar before last call.

When looking for lasting love, forget what looks right, forget what you think should be right, and forget what your friends, parents, or other people think is right, and ask yourself: Does the relationship feel right to me?

The dating game can be nerve-wracking. It's only natural to worry about how you'll come across and whether or not your date will like you. But no matter how shy or socially awkward you feel, you can overcome your nerves and self-consciousness and forge a great connection.

Focus outward, not inward. To combat first-date nerves, focus your attention on what your date is saying and doing and what's going on around you, rather than on your internal thoughts. Staying fully present in the moment will help take your mind off worries and insecurities. Be curious. When you're truly curious about someone else's thoughts, feelings, experiences, stories, and opinions, it shows—and they'll like you for it. You'll come across as far more attractive and interesting than if you spend your time trying to promote yourself to your date. And if you aren't genuinely interested in your date, there's little point in pursuing the relationship further.

Now, go change your profile and make yourself more swipe-worthy! But above all have fun and stay safe.

GLOSSARY

Glossary & Terminology Guide

If you've ever been in the dating game, you'll probably have at least one disastrous tale to tell. This book is full of them. The whole process can be exhausting and confusing: the constant 'are we/aren't we?'; the 'I like them, but I don't know if they like me'; the 'I don't know what they want' . . . it goes on. And now with online dating applications taking the world by storm, meeting a romantic partner in the traditional *offline* sense is becoming more and more uncommon.

However, the good news is that there are terms to help you decipher those age-old dating issues within a modern-day context (cue for you to read back through your old texts to analyse what the true meaning of those abbreviations meant). I hope you find them useful.

Aromantic

Aromanticism is rare, but it is real. A certain portion of the population does not experience the feelings of romantic love that seem to come naturally to so many of us. While that might seem like either a blessing or a curse, depending on your take on love, perhaps the most significant hurdle for aromantic people is simply feeling left out and misunderstood by a culture for whom dating, love, and marriage are not only the norm, but the de facto expectation for all.

Asexual

Being asexual doesn't specify whom you're attracted to; instead, I means that you don't experience sexual attraction. But this doesn't mean you can't have sex—only that you don't feel the need in the same way. While dating an asexual person, expect to check in regularly with them regarding their desires and boundaries, just as you would when dating anybody else.

Big Dick Energy

Big dick energy, or BDE, is something only a small amount of people possess. It's the quality of having supreme confidence without needing to be loud or controlling—it is a quiet understanding of who you are and what you bring to the table that doesn't require backtalk, bragging, or bulls#@!. In short, someone with BDE is incredibly hot, and more guys should try to emulate that. The truth is, you can have BDE no matter what your genital size is as long as you're comfortable being who you are.

Breadcrumbing

The coward's way of what is already a coward's way out. Unlike a ghoster, who will cease all communication completely, a breadcrumber will send flirtatious but non-committal texts like 'Hey, what's up?' without ever trying to meet up. It could go on for months, even years. For the breadcrumber, it's an easy way to string someone along and keep the door open should they decide to pursue something down the line or to make you so desperate that you agree to be a booty call. Sometimes, the breadcrumber will disappear for weeks, only to resurface and throw another mystery crumb your way, leading you to tear your hair out, wondering whether they are interested after all.

Benching

Similar to breadcrumbing, benching involves stringing someone along just enough to keep them around as an option. Breadcrumbing is different from benching in that it's crueler because the victim doesn't know if you're just being flaky or if you're not that interested. With benching, it's clearer that the bencher is pursuing other avenues and just putting you on the bench in case one of their main players gets called off the field.

Catfish

A person who uses someone else's pictures and profile to lure interest but hides their own identity. The person you think you are chatting with is not showing their true identity.

Catch and Release

This describes someone who loves to chase, but when they've 'caught' a person they let them go with 'ghosting' intent.

Collector

Someone who collects matches but has no intention of ever engaging in conversation and/or in meeting up.

Curving

Getting curved is a little easier to bear than a flat-out rejection. It's when someone turns down your advances but doesn't do it in a direct way. A great example is when Drake tried to kiss Rihanna on stage at the 2016 VMAs award, and she literally curved to give him the cheek. While curving is somewhat nicer than a lot of other items on this list, it's still often used as a way of keeping an option open even if you're not really that interested.

Cushioning

You meet someone you really like, but they are already in a relationship. The way they flirt with you via text makes it seem like they are interested, but they make no indication that they're planning on leaving their current partner. This is cushioning, aka the act of keeping the seat warm in case they want to use it somewhere down the line.

DTR

DTR is an acronym for 'define the relationship'. You may have been dating someone for a while and it is now time to determine and define what you are to each other and where the relationship is heading.

Fire-dooring

This is when one person has all the power in an exchange. Someone who will text you but fail to respond when you text back. Someone who will never make plans to see you but expect you to drop everything and come over when they happen to have a free afternoon. As the name implies, this is not a two-way street. It's a fire door. You can get out, but you can't get back in.

Fuckboy

Ah, the fuckboy. It's a boy vs (gentle)man situation; they may be 'nice' to girls but don't actually treat them right at all. These womanizers may not have *actual* girlfriends but their actions still cause heartbreak.

Ghosting

You meet someone, go on a date, have a great time. You text back and forth, then you send them a text one day and don't get a response. You wait a few days, thinking that they are probably just busy. Then weeks go by and you realize that whatever you had is over. It's bad enough that people do this after dates, what's even more appalling is that I know people who have experienced this in relationships. You're seeing someone for months, then, one day, they just vanish into thin air.

Haunting

This is something that makes my eyes roll. It is when the person who once 'ghosted' you returns to your cyber sphere in a lurking sort of way. It's the classic unexpected 'hello stranger' effect, but through social media—they'll like your post on Facebook or are always the first to view your Snapchat story. Just like the cowardly art of 'ghosting', when someone is 'haunting' you they don't get in touch with you directly.

Kittenfishing

We've all heard of catfishing, in which someone pretends to be someone they're not in order to catch a potential mate. In 'kittenfishing', however, someone isn't exorbitantly lying in their online dating profile, they're just stretching the truth. The most basic version of this involves posting old or heavily altered photos, or lying about weight or height, so that the person who walks into the bar only vaguely resembles the person you matched with.

No One Night Stand (NOS)

Commonly seen now on ladies' profile statements, this can be both positive and negative, depending on the context. It means what it says. Not interested to meet for one night of fun, in the physical sense. Conversely, its absence can also be interpreted as being open to that type of encounter.

No Strings Attached (NSA)

Again, this usage can be both positive and negative—meaning the person is either accepting or against having an encounter or relationship with conditions. Often used to state that the individual is looking for a physical relationship with no expectations of it turning into a close, long-term relationship.

Orbiting

This is a new, terrible trend in dating. In orbiting, a person will ghost you, but continue to stalk your social media. You wouldn't know this is happening with Facebook or Twitter, but Instagram stories and Snapchat tell you which users have watched your content. If your 'ghoster' appears, that means you are being orbited. This can lead to psychological anguish for the victim too, as they wonder if it means the 'ghoster' is regretting their decision to abandon you, or simply keeping themselves in your orbit so that you don't forget about them completely in the off-chance they feel like hooking up again. Of course, you will never know, because they don't have the courtesy to tell you how they feel. The alternative term for this breakdown of basic courtesy is 'haunting'.

Pen-paling

Someone who matches but wants to engage in endless messaging and has no intention to meet in person. Often such people are looking for friendship and/or could be people hiding their identity.

Polyamorous

Being 'poly' means that you can be in a relationship while enjoying relationships with other people. The key here is communication and honesty and taking great care to make sure you're not hurting or betraying any of your partners. It's been around in some form as far back as Ancient Rome but is having a resurgence in popularity.

Roaching

You find out your partner hasn't cheated on you but has been casually looking for someone else on the side. And instead of accepting guilt, they then shift the blame on you by saying that they didn't realize you were monogamous. This is roaching, and as the term implies, it is not a nice thing to do.

Slow Fade

The 'slow fade' is when someone gradually cuts you off. They may start to interact with you less and less and stop making any efforts at all, so that eventually you are no longer in contact. Not great, but a little bit less brutal than 'ghosting'? Or, maybe not.

Stashing

You're dating someone, and you feel like it's going well. But you notice that they don't feature you in any of their social media, or de-tag themselves from any posts you put up. This is the modern version of getting weird when you ask to meet your partner's parents. The person you're with is into you, but they aren't sure they want to close the door on other possibilities, and therefore 'stash you' as one would with a basket of dirty laundry, in the closet.

Submarining

This is when someone breaks up with you or ghosts you and then just pops back into your life after a lengthy silence as though nothing had happened. Torpedo that thing!

Talking

When people are dating but describe it as 'talking', they are commitment-phobes who want to keep it casual. This is great if it is mutual, but otherwise it can be rather frustrating.

Tuning

'Tuning' can often be hard to recognize and can be mistaken for 'benching'. However, the intent is very different; in this case, the person does want the relationship to progress and continue but they aren't upfront about it. So, if someone likes all of your Instagram photos, sends you Snapchats of their dog, and use emojis in their sweet-but-vague texts, they may be flirting but are afraid to give too much of themselves in case things between you don't materialize. 'Tuning' can be frustrating and prolonged, but usually the person is doing the groundwork before asking you on a date.

Warehouse

This is when the person doing the 'tuning' is already in a relationship. They may want to get out of their current situation, but they aren't ready or committed to do so. So, in the meantime they 'tune' other people as a sort of insurance to gain affirmation and interest in case they were to exit their current relationship. Hence, they put you in the 'warehouse'. Not exactly cheating per se, but definitely not nice.

Zombieing

This is the latest term you need to add to your dating dictionary. Essentially, it is when your ex 'comes back from the dead' and pops back into your life after a spell of acting like a stranger—something pretty much all of us would have experienced with an ex, in one way or another.

BOOK THREE

16 Swipes All Pride

I have started to pen the final book in this series. I have shared my own view in *16 SWIPES No Breakfast*, the ladies' perspective in this book, and in closing, the LGBTQ *16 SWIPES All Pride*.

We are all unique, special, and deserve to be loved. So, what is it like for a male or female and those in between to find a partner? This is a topic that requires sensitivity, understanding, and acceptance. It also requires humour as without it, life is dull. What follows are a few stories that I hope will whet your appetite to read the book when it's completed.

To set some context, when looking for a straight partner do men and women look for the same things as gay men and women?

In the 1950s, Dr Evelyn Hooker studied thirty homosexual males and thirty heterosexual males from all walks of life. The two groups were matched for age, IQ, social environment, and education. Dr Hooker administered three projective tests: the Rorschach test, in which people describe what they see in abstract ink blots; the Thematic Apperception Test (TAT); and the Make-A-Picture-Story (MAPS) Test, in which people tell stories about different pictures to measure patterns of thoughts, attitudes, and emotions respectively. Unaware of each subject's sexual orientation, two independent Rorschach experts evaluated the men's overall adjustment using a five-point scale. They classified two-thirds of the heterosexuals and two-thirds of the homosexuals in the three highest categories of adjustment. When asked to identify which Rorschach protocols were obtained from homosexuals, the experts could not distinguish respondents' sexual orientation at a level better than chance. A third expert used the TAT and MAPS protocols to evaluate the psychological adjustment of the men. As with the Rorschach responses, the adjustment ratings of the homosexual and heterosexuals did not differ significantly. Based on these findings, Dr Hooker tentatively suggested that homosexuals were as psychologically normal as heterosexuals.

So, there you have it, in general terms, we are all the same psychologically. I'm told that such a research was also carried out on thirty women many years later, with the same outcome. The research was the first to empirically test the assumption that gay men and women were mentally unhealthy and maladjusted. The fact that no differences were found between gay and straight participants sparked more research in this area and began to dismantle the myth that homosexual men and women are inherently unhealthy.

The conclusion, we all swipe the same way even if we are from the LGBTQ spectrum.

The first story I will recount is about Kai, an American-born Asian male in his thirties and living in Los Angeles. It was fascinating account to hear.

Kai started by sharing that whenever he viewed the Tinder profile of a tall, dark, and handsome man in tight fitting swimwear, he liked him. The same goes for when he observed a tattooed man in a jumper. He also liked women in tight black dresses or beachwear. As someone who identifies as bisexual, Kai enjoyed being able to connect with both men and women on Tinder. But he clarified that it didn't mean he connected with everyone in the same way. He commented that perhaps Tinder should develop an app that better allows its subscribers to express their sexual orientation and preferences. He then shared something that was interesting. He had experienced first-hand how the world of men seeking men on Tinder. He pointed out how things can become a little like shopping in a meat market, but went on to say that it was still better than any gay-specific dating app he had used. Kai wanted a long-term relationship, and not overnight flings. His biggest challenge, being bisexual, was that he wanted to just talk to men and women and not be judged. In essence who cares what orientation you are, if you click you click.

Many gay men he believes look for a partner in the wrong place. While heading to the bondage party at a leather bar dressed in only a thong, will undoubtedly lead to a fun night, but that night probably won't turn into something more. Kai also shared that in his experience, with gay-specific hook-up apps if you've said less than 100 words before getting naked together, then don't expect it to turn into something serious. (Again, that's not to say it's impossible, but let's keep expectations realistic.)

To know the rest, watch out for the book!

Acknowledgments

Firstly, I thank the 16 very special ladies—who shall, of course, remain anonymous—for allowing me to share their personal stories, sharing with me the journey of crafting this book, and nurturing my understanding and ability to honour the female perspective. Equally, I thank the seven ladies who also added some extra flare by sharing their personal experiences. In fact, they were so good that I simply had to include their stories in this book as bonus chapters.

I thank my daughter, Freya, for her continued love and appreciation, even though I have not always been there in body but always in spirit. You are my world. The challenge of being a parent has allowed me to understand the struggles my parents faced and helped me to love them more. Being a father myself has shown me the way to understand and love my own father more deeply, despite him being in the clouds now. He rests in peace along with my mother in the grounds of Dartmouth Castle in England—a rugged and beautiful spot by the sea that is so befitting for them both.

I thank my late father and mother for their loving efforts to raise a family of two very troublesome boys. I thank my oldest brother, Richard, for understanding my sentiments and admiring my words. It's been too long brother since we've shared a beer and a bag of crisps in an English pub garden, just like we did when we were young boys . . . maybe not the beer back in the day—more a bottle of coke and a soggy paper straw.

I thank my editor Lina Jacobs, whose help, brilliant creativity, and enthusiasm have guided this book from its conception to its completion. I thank my publisher Nora from Penguin Random House for her ceaseless trust in my work and for putting up with my occasional delays in submission. Sometimes writing takes longer than we think it should.

I also thank the staff at Penguin Random House for their continued responsiveness to my needs. We writers can be needy, and our egos, at times, need taming.

I thank all the women who participated in the research I conducted for this book. Though their stories are not in this book, they offered advice and encouraged me to write this book. Their positive and loving feedback has supported me in authoring this simple presentation of such a complex subject.

I thank my social media followers, supporters, fans, and readers who have been so loyal. I write so that you may enjoy it. Nothing gives me more pleasure than to bleed ink, knowing you value my work. I also thank my critics, for, without you, I would not improve.

Mark Powell, 2020